American Business and
the Quick Fix

AMERICAN BUSINESS
and the
QUICK FIX

Michael E. McGill, Ph.D.

HENRY HOLT AND COMPANY
New York

Published by Henry Holt and Company, Inc.,
115 West 18th Street, New York, New York 10011.
Published in Canada by Fitzhenry & Whiteside Limited,
195 Allstate Parkway, Markham, Ontario L3R 4T8.

Library of Congress Cataloging-in-Publication Data
McGill, Michael E.
American business and the quick fix.
Includes index.
1. Industrial management—United States.   2. Fads—
United States.   3. Organizational effectiveness.
I. Title.
HD70.U5M35   1988   658′.00973   87-28692

ISBN 0-8050-0786-5

First Edition

Designed by Kate Nichols
Printed in the United States of America
1 3 5 7 9 10 8 6 4 2

ISBN 0-8050-0786-5

At every management level myths exist to answer questions that no one had thought to ask. Myths reflect imagined constraints and objectives chosen by habit. The perceiver of myths discovers in them unexpected opportunities to create the future.

—Martin Starr,
Operations Management

Contents

Acknowledgments

The idea for this book emerged from the business acumen of Jane Pasenen, who generously shared her executive experiences with me. My agent, Dominick Abel, helped to shape and guide the project throughout, offering needed personal and professional support.

I am indebted to my colleagues in the Department of Organization Behavior at the Edwin L. Cox School of Business, Southern Methodist University, for their tutelage. John Slocum and Mike Wooton have been particularly helpful. I have learned a great deal from my good friends and consulting colleagues Tom Hofstedt and Rick Ross. My learning debt extends to the hundreds of managers and students of management who have shared their experiences with me over my twenty-year career as a professor and consultant. I want to acknowledge particularly my friends at "the Farm" and "the Treehouse" for the many ways in which they have enhanced my understanding of the challenges of management.

My secretary, Elizabeth Wisakowsky, has provided support and service far beyond what her duties call for. Her logistical skills have made it possible for me to juggle teaching, consulting, administering, and writing. She has always had the right word or action to move things forward; without her this book might never have been brought to completion.

Nadine Hill typed the manuscript with speed, accuracy, and the attention to detail of a true professional.

Finally, I want to express my heartfelt thanks to Marian Wood. Marian is that unlikely publishing-world combination of editor and friend. She brings to her work a critical mind and a caring heart, and she makes me better than I am. I could not ask for more from an editor or friend, and I feel truly blessed to have both in one.

I sincerely express my gratitude to all those who have contributed so much to this project. I alone remain responsible for the conclusions I have drawn.

American Business and
the Quick Fix

1

Introduction: Myth and the Modern Manager

In 1776, Adam Smith in *The Wealth of Nations* argued that efficiency in business results from specialization and division of labor. For the next 200 years, economists, organization theorists, management philosophers, financial analysts, management scientists, consultants, and practitioners toiled diligently but in relative obscurity with the complex question of what makes organizations effective. Few among the general public have heard of Frederick Taylor, Henri Fayol, Frank and Lillian Gilbreth—key organization thinkers during the early part of the century. Elton Mayo, Frederick Rothlisberger, and Chester Barnard, mentors to millions of managers in the 1930s and the 1940s, are hardly household names. Even more contemporary contributors to thinking about management—Alfred Chandler, Rensis Likert, Douglas McGregor, Herbert Simon—are unknown even to the majority of those in business.

But all of this began changing a decade ago. Today, effectiveness, productivity, efficiency are as topical as the latest fad diet. Mention "Excellence" or "The One-Minute Manager" and most everyone knows what you're talking about. Formerly obscure

1

management theorists and consultants are now best-selling authors and talk-show guests. Chief executive officers, such as Lee Iacocca of Chrysler and Ross Perot of GM-EDS, are our new culture heroes, regularly making the covers of popular magazines. What does it all mean? Does it mean anything at all?

In 1985, I began giving my MBA students, management seminar participants, and consulting clients the following test:*

Forty Years of Famous Fads and Fixes

For each of the forty fads or fixes below, identify the decade—the 1950s, 1960s, 1970s, 1980s—or the particular year of their zenith.

_____ Zero-Based Budgets

_____ Nehru Jackets

_____ Pac Man

_____ Theory Z

_____ Theory Y

_____ Davy Crockett

_____ Happy Faces

_____ MBWA

_____ MBAs

_____ MBO

_____ The Twist

_____ T-Groups/Sensitivity
Training

_____ Streaking

_____ Downsizing

_____ Go-Go Boots

_____ Quantitative Methods
(PERT/CPM)

_____ Rubik's Cube

_____ Hula Hoops

_____ Matrix Management

_____ Intrapreneuring/
Skunkworks

_____ One Minute
Management

_____ Tie-Dying

_____ Computerization

_____ Mood Rings

_____ Conglomeration

_____ Corporate Culture

_____ Phone Booth/VW
Stuffing

_____ Slinky

_____ Managerial Grid

_____ 3-D Movies

_____ Participative
Management

_____ Pet Rocks

_____ Trivial Pursuit

_____ Portfolio Management

*Answers can be found in the Appendix, p. 223.

_____ Psychedelic Designs   _____ Poodle Skirts
_____ Hot Pants   _____ Centralization
_____ Diversification   _____ Swatches

After administering this quiz to respondents of every age and occupation, I have observed that there is more to be learned from the reactions of respondents than there is from the accuracy of their responses.

MBA students are predictably befuddled by the juxtaposition of pop culture phenomena they have heard of as history but haven't experienced (Nehru jackets and mood rings are beyond their ken) with topics from their current MBA curricula. They have studied One-minute management and corporate culture. Additionally, there are many things on the list that sound like something they ought to recognize but don't—zero-based budgets and PERT/CPM. For these students, typically in their mid to late twenties, the fads and fixes of the eighties have the character of fixtures in their lives. In their eyes, Trivial Pursuit will have the staying power of Monopoly, and portfolio management is a corporate commandment. They don't know why fads and fixes of the 1950s, 1960s, and 1970s were so fleeting, but they are adamant that the same fortune will not befall the popular culture and management of the 1980s. With the conviction that can come only from youth, one twenty-five-year-old MBA asserts, "Our generation is different, we're more stable. What's here today is here to stay!"

Middle-aged middle- and upper-middle managers are typically a much more seasoned (and cynical) lot. In their careers they have seen many fads and fixes come and go. They look upon a list that includes streaking, downsizing, go-go boots, and PERT with a nonchalance born of experience. "Twenty years ago we wore tie-dyed jeans to company-sponsored T-groups; yesterday I wore my MBWA gimme-cap to a quality circle meeting." This manager from a major electronics firm went on to say, "When you look at all the stuff we've been into and out of over the years you realize the key is not to take any of it too seriously."

3

Not all mid-life, mid-career middle managers are so philosophical about the fads-and-fixes list; some use it as fodder for their cynicism about corporate capriciousness. A real estate development leasing manager describes how she and her peers view fads and fixes. "It describes everything we've done in the thirteen years I've been here. We joke about the owners as being charter members of the Management-of-the-Month Club. If it's the thing to do, we do it until the next thing to do comes along."

Higher up the corporate ladder, senior executives, company presidents, division VPs, and general managers tend to look upon this exercise with neither the wonderment of MBA students nor the whimsy of middle managers. These seasoned corporate citizens, who in their personal lives scoff at the idea of fad diets or no-money-down real estate schemes, don't see the parallels in their own fascination with fleeting formulas for business success. For them, the management of the moment is serious business. Many of these executives have spent millions of dollars, not to mention man-hours, on implementing these "magical" techniques over the years. They do not take kindly to their investments being compared to the likes of pet rocks and mood rings. Some of this reaction may emanate from the embarrassing realization that the Slinky has outlived any of the magical managerial techniques of the 1950s. (In testimony to the observation that all things come full circle, the Slinky is now a demonstration device in one of the newest management fads, "visionary leadership.") The general manager of a tire manufacturer defended his company's reputation for "management by best-seller": "It's ludicrous to compare what our company and lots of other companies have done to hula hoops. We gave a lot of thought to each of the programs we've been involved in. The fact that we weren't in any of them very long just means that something better came along and we were smart enough to see it." Experienced executives can and do speak of the value of experimentation. They frequently cite the handful of management fads that have made it into the managerial mainstream over the last forty years. But the facts about fads speak even louder. For all practical purposes, zero-based budgets are as obsolete as Nehru jackets.

4

Other executives argue that the fads have disappeared because they have been integrated into everyday organizational practices. "We don't recognize them because they are all around us!" This sounds suspiciously like the old joke about walking backward to ward off elephants. Does it work? You don't see any elephants around here, do you?

Is "Forty Years of Famous Fads and Fixes" a history lesson, a cynical comparison, an executive embarrassment? What you see in the list probably will depend on your own experience of these fads and fixes over the last forty years. If you haven't been around management for that long, you might relate more easily to the following list culled from the past two years of *Business Week*, which reports on the ins and outs in recent business fads.

What's In	*What's Out*
Intrapreneurs	Corporate planners
Pay for performance	Management by objectives
Executive celebrities	Autocratic bosses
Demassing	Walk-around managing
Skunkworks	Factory of the future
Restructuring	Theory Z
Back to basics	Consultants
Corporate culture	Synergy
Vision	Strategic planning
Global corporations	Domestic corporations
Cash compensation	Stock options
Cost control	Vice-presidents
Security	Risk
Engineers	MBAs
Quality	Quantity
Laptop computers	Mainframes

Lists of the "ins and outs" or "fads and fixes" are entertaining, but they can and should be educational as well. We ought to garner from them a profound sense of perspective about popular management panaceas.

Fads and fixes emerge from the myths of management and, in

turn, they promote the same myths. The result is a managerial morass wherein simplistic solutions take form, flower briefly, then sink back to feed new forms. So long as management stays mired in its own mythic-ridden marshland, effective substantive solutions will elude managers, trapped as they are by their own imagined constraints and by objectives chosen by habit. There is no firm footing in the modern myths, no bedrock on which to build business, only quick fixes. Only when managers can recognize the myths for what they are can they set aside fads, establish a firm foothold on solid ground, and begin to lay the foundation for better business practices. It is the purpose of this book to expose the modern management myths, to show where they have led and where they have led astray, to make of managers "perceivers of myths" and, in the process, discoverers of opportunities to create the future.

2

Forty Years of Fads and Fixes

A fad is something that everyone wants today and
no one wants tomorrow.
—*Overheard at the Second Annual*
Fad Fair, Detroit, 1986

Managerial magic in one form or another is as ancient as organizations themselves. An instruction book for Egyptian leaders in 2000 B.C. advised on how to communicate with a subordinate: "Do not rebuff him before he has said that for which he came." Moses used the principle of span of control in preparing for the exodus from Egypt: For every ten workers a foreman, for every ten foremen a supervisor, and so on. The result was the pyramidal structure. Niccolo Machiavelli was a sixteenth-century consultant of sorts, and he assembled his advice on how to gain and use power in *The Prince*.

These antecedents notwithstanding, it was not until 1911 that the first of the management fixers as we know them today appeared on the scene in the person of Frederick W. Taylor, widely regarded as the father of scientific management.

There is much about the work of Taylor that qualified him as the first of the famous fixers. To begin with, he had a very simple view of the manager's role. It was "knowing exactly what you want men to do, and then seeing they do it in the best and cheapest way." Drawing on his engineering background, Taylor de-

7

vised simple formulas for managing that were based on standards, work measurements (time-and-motion studies), and piece-rate pay scales. All of this advice he made available in a book, *The Principles of Scientific Management,* which he promoted in his lectures around the country, much like the speakers on the management seminar circuit today. So widely regarded was Taylor's work that Congress debated mandatory scientific management methods for the railroads. This would be akin today to the Defense Department requiring contractors to adopt the eight Elements of Excellence. (In 1986, the army did mandate training based on *In Search of Excellence* for its civilian personnel.)

Others soon followed in Taylor's consulting tracks. Henri Fayol, a French mining engineer, proposed fourteen principles for managers to follow. Two executives with General Motors, James D. Mooney and Alan C. Reilly, teamed together in 1931 to co-author *Onward Industry* and spread the word about the universal principles of management discovered at GM (shades of Iacocca). In 1938, the president of New Jersey Bell, Chester I. Barnard, wrote his classic *The Functions of the Executive.*

All of this has a ring of familiarity to it. Consultants and successful executives reduce their managerial experiences and insights to simple, universal formulas and principles, which they promote in books and lecture tours. This could just as well be a description of the events in management over the last five years instead of the nascent years of management nearly a century ago.

The pattern was set by these pioneering fixers but fewer and fewer in management today can relate to this distant perspective. The lessons to be learned from our fascination with quick fixes are best gleaned from experiences closer to us.

In 1941, James Burnham (in his landmark book, *The Managerial Revolution*) identified managers as "the class which is in the process of becoming the ruling class of society." Ten years later, Burnham's foresight became fact when America discovered the profession of management. The post–World War II productivity boom generated thousands of new jobs and these, in turn, spawned a new organization layer of overseers who, unlike their predecessors—supervisors and foremen—did no direct work themselves but rather managed those who managed workers.

America in the 1950s was fascinated with this new organizational creature—the white-collar class, the managerial class. Novelists used managers as protagonists: Tom Rath in Sloan Wilson's *Man in the Gray Flannel Suit;* John Galt in *Atlas Shrugged,* by Ayn Rand; Cameron Hawley's Dan Walling in *Executive Suite.* Broadway saw a blockbuster corporate musical comedy in Shepard Mead's *How to Succeed in Business Without Really Trying.* In his best-selling *The Organization Man,* sociologist William F. Whyte asked the questions that were on everyone's mind: Who are the managers? How are they selected? What do they do? How do they do it? But the decade was not without its doubters: Was management a skill, an art, a profession? Or a scam? Still, too many had too much invested to let such doubts linger for long. There was a rush to legitimate management as a worthy pursuit. Managers and the teachers of managers—universities and colleges, many of whom started business schools to capture some of the GI bill money—were particularly quick to defend their newfound territory. They argued that management was a profession like medicine or the law, with all of the attendant requirements.

In a profession, decisions are made by means of general principles, theories, or propositions that are independent of the particular case under consideration. In management, it was argued, there are certain principles of how to handle people, money, information, and so on that are independent of any particular business or company. Professions are also characterized by expertise in specific areas. The emerging business schools of America were only too eager to establish such areas in their curricula: accounting, finance, industrial relations, marketing, and so forth. In so doing, they created their own market.

Professionals are supposed to be objective, making decisions independent of sentiment and self-interest. Managers in the 1950s aspired to this level of personal detachment. A completely rational decision maker able to make choices based on calculation rather than on emotion was the managerial ideal.

Finally, in true professions, individuals achieve status by accomplishment, not by inherent qualities such as birth order, relationship to people in power, race, religion, or ethnic origin. The democratic character of the managerial profession was particularly appealing to America's new aspiring middle class. It meant that any man could be a manager.

These professional posturings notwithstanding, there remained a great deal of uncertainty among newly anointed managers, who wondered just what it was they were supposed to do and just how they were supposed to do it. Somehow the managerial mystique that was so captivating didn't have much to say about technique. Enter the fixers of the 1950s who found in formulas a way to further the managerial mystique *through* technique.

The "formula fifties" in management really was not the fault of Peter Drucker (though he has often taken credit for it, and countless others have assigned him blame). It just *seems* as though he caused it all because his formulation, management by objectives, or MBO, is the fifties fix most remembered by managers. In *The Practice of Management* (1954), Drucker argued for a philosophy of management based on uniting organizational objectives with employees' personal objectives. MBO was to be a simple, three-step process: (1) The manager and the subordinate jointly determine the subordinate's specific areas of responsibility. An essential part of this process is mutual agreement about the tasks to be accomplished. (2) The manager and the subordinate agree on the priorities and standards of performance for each area of responsibility. (3) The manager and the subordinate agree on a general work plan for achieving the desired results in each broad area of responsibility—the results tying in with the overall objectives of the organization or unit.[1]

MBO was just one of the magical management formulas of the 1950s, all of which had to do with reducing the processes of management to measurable activities. Management *science*, operations *research, quantitative* management were the driving forces of the time. All of these techniques were aided by the widespread availability of mainframe computers, which rendered the heretofore incalculable eminently calculable.

Nowhere was the formula focus of management in the 1950s more in evidence than in PERT/CPM. In 1957–58, the U.S. Navy developed a new system to plan, schedule, and control the development of the Polaris submarine. The system, program evaluation and review technique/critical path management, consisted of four steps: (1) identifying all activities; (2) estimating time required to complete each activity; (3) ordering the sequence of activities around *events* or points at which an activity begins or ends; (4) identifying the critical path, the longest set of adjoining activities. The navy credited PERT/CPM with enabling the completion of the Polaris two years ahead of time despite the complexity of coordinating 250 prime contractors, over 9,000 subcontractors, and hundreds of thousands of individuals. Of course, computers were used to calculate the thousands of events and interactions and to monitor the CPM.

Systems such as MBO and PERT/CPM epitomized the formula fifties in management. Thousands of companies rushed to implement MBO and PERT programs and other equivalent techniques in management science, all supported by mathematical models, mainframe computers, and forms. Oh, yes, the forms. Ultimately, it was the forms that were blamed for the failure of formulas in the 1950s—the substance of many techniques was suffocated by the sheer weight of the paperwork required by the systems. Donald N. Frey, chief executive of Bell and Howell, recalls his exposure to PERT as a young manager at Ford: "We went to Wright-Patterson Air Force Base, where they had PERT charting down to a science. They had more guys working on PERT charts than they had doing the job. It was an enormous overhead cost just to allow the generals to show visitors their PERT charts." Undaunted, Ford implemented the system throughout the company. "We all did them. But it took so much effort to get the charts done, you might as well have spent the time getting the job done." The same was said to be true of MBO—form overtook function, leading most managers to conclude that the paperwork involved in the process ended up consuming more time than the proposed benefits were worth.

Of course, it wasn't really paperwork that proved to be the undoing of MBO, PERT, and the other alphabetical jargon of the 1950s. Paperwork merely provided a convenient scapegoat for managers, a way to explain away the failure of formulas to produce the promised managerial magic without faulting the formula or their own understanding or execution of it. In truth, the formulas failed because they were *too* simple. It became increasingly evident that rote advice and computerized calculations simply could not accommodate the complexities of managing people. MBO provides an effective illustration.

The "ideal" MBO process should proceed in five steps: (1) individual discussion with his superior of the subordinate's description of his own job; (2) establishment of short-term performance targets; (3) meetings with the superior to discuss progress toward targets; (4) establishment of checkpoints to measure progress; (5) discussion between superior and subordinate at the end of a defined period to assess the results of the subordinate's efforts.

In practice, managers trying to use MBO encountered many difficulties. Job descriptions and pre-established performance targets are static statements that do not give appropriate weight to the need for flexibility and discretion, especially in higher-level managerial jobs. In addition, MBO could not deal adequately with the interdependent nature of jobs. Finally, MBO argued for performance appraisals that would counsel employees, but managers typically have difficulty with appraisals of any type and employees mostly want to know if it's going to be linked to pay. In short, MBO was a simple, popular solution that, once put to the test, did not meet managers' needs *and*, to make matters worse, took a tremendous amount of paperwork to accomplish.

Toward the end of the 1950s, formula fixes were on the wane. Managers had become disenchanted with the science of management and the techniques thereof that seemed ill-suited to the social and human demands of management. Managers had been through MBO, PERT/CPM, etc., and literally were at the end of the alphabet when they found the fix that would take them into the "sensitive sixties"—Theory Y.

In 1960, Douglas McGregor wrote *The Human Side of Enterprise*. He asserted that managers could make one of two sets of assumptions about workers, each of which led to a different view of how to manage.

Theory X assumptions:		
	1.	People do not like work and try to avoid it.
	2.	People do not like work, so managers have to control, direct, coerce, and threaten employees to get them to work toward organizational goals.
	3.	People prefer to be directed, to avoid responsibility; they want security; they have little ambition.

Theory Y assumptions:		
	1.	People do not naturally dislike work; work is a natural part of their lives.
	2.	People are internally motivated to reach objectives to which they are committed.
	3.	People are committed to goals to the degree that they receive personal rewards when they reach their objectives.
	4.	People will both seek and accept responsibility under favorable conditions.
	5.	People have the capacity to be innovative in solving organizational problems.

6. People are bright, but under most organizational conditions their potentials are underutilized.[2]

McGregor argued that Theory X assumptions about people were outdated, that performance among an educated and responsible work force was based more on internal than on external (management science) controls. All managers needed to do was to allow people to exercise their natural responsibility and satisfy some of their personal needs. After a decade of memorizing formulas, filling out forms, and calculating everything that moved, managers were much relieved to discover that it was all much simpler than that—all they really had to do was to be "people-oriented." The question was, How? Enter the fixers.

In the 1960s, thousands of managers from America's largest and most successful companies—IBM, TRW, Texas Instruments, Weyerhaeuser, Rockwell, and most of the rest of the *Fortune* 500—went off in small groups to seek self-awareness and sensitivity. Sensitivity training, laboratory training, T-groups, encounter groups were the names most often associated with these popular learning activities. Meeting in small groups of ten to sixteen managers, for anywhere from a weekend marathon to a two-week residential program, the objectives of the T-group were to help managers become aware of why they and others behave as they do in groups. This was done with the help of a "trainer," whose job was to create an atmosphere in which the motivations for typical behavior, of which managers were presumed often to be unaware, were brought to the surface in exaggerated form.

T-groups are best remembered by managers for the activities used to create the necessary "freeing" atmosphere. Nonverbal exercises were very popular. Foot-massaging, blindfolded "trust" walks, crawling around like animals—all were commonplace. One electronics executive reports his experience: "First we took off our shoes, then we paired off and faced our partners from opposite sides of the room. Next we were told to run at each other as fast as we could! After the collisions, we were supposed to talk about what we felt. Looking back on it now, I'm struck by three things. One, no one was hurt. Two, we actually did what we were told. And three, the company spent a fortune on that sort of bullshit!"

Most major corporations exposed their top managers to some form of sensitivity training in the early 1960s and many extended the program far down into the ranks. The presumed advantage was that managers would learn about themselves from the "feedback" from their peers and become more sensitive to their employees, more Theory Y. The goals were laudable but the consequences were often lamentable.

At the very least, the connection between the activities in T-groups and the requirements of jobs was often obscure. Managers had trouble transferring their weekend awareness into Monday-morning job performance. At the worst, T-groups touched on deeply personal issues and raised serious questions about the relationship between an individual's personal life and his/her organizational life. The fad was eventually discarded by many managers because it simply seemed too foolish. Others lost faith because it smacked of psychotherapy. In the main, however, sensitivity training lost favor with managers because it seemed to have so little connection to managers' jobs.

One fad of the sensitive sixties that was closer to the mainstream of management was the Managerial Grid. Promulgated by Robert R. Blake and Jane S. Mouton in their 1964 book, *The Managerial Grid*, "participative management" became *the* way to manage in the 1960s. The concept behind participative management was that "team" managers could maximally emphasize their concern for people and their concern for production.[3] In short, by getting participation, managers could have the best of both worlds—X and Y, productivity and sensitivity—with ultimately improved profitability, increased job satisfaction, fewer grievances, and virtually everything else a manager might aspire to.

The participative fad turned on the "Grid," a test that categorized managers by their preferred style (impoverished; country club; task; middle-of-the-road; and team), and plotted a path toward making them participative managers. Few managers in the 1960s escaped exposure to some form of the Grid. Many organizations bought the entire six-phase Grid organization development program, which committed them to ten to fifteen years of pursuing participation. Some companies that started with the program in the sixties aren't done yet. As one executive of an educational services firm notes: "Every now and then I'll look at all of those Grid materials on my bookshelf and wonder whatever happened to the program? We didn't make a conscious decision to stop, it just sort of faded away."

The participative fad did indeed fade as managers realized that being a participative manager was costly and not always more effective. Team management proved to be time-consuming and conflict-generating, and it demanded considerable social skills on the part of everyone involved. In many companies, the pursuit of participation actually distracted from organizational goals. Still, these costs would have been willingly incurred by businesses if the results were measurably better, but most often the results did not justify the cost. An aerospace executive observed, "What we learned about participation was that if no one knew what was going on, the group had a better chance of finding a solution than any individual member. It's the blind-squirrel phenomenon. Even a blind squirrel finds an acorn once in a while. It makes sense that a group of blind squirrels will find an acorn sooner than one blind squirrel looking on his own. On the other hand, if one squirrel in the group can see, then the rest of the squirrels would be better off sitting in the tree and waiting for him to bring back the nuts. Participation too often forces the expert into the position of having to convince everyone that he can see. In our business a lot of the real experts aren't too socially adept, and forcing them into a participative situation runs the risk of minimizing the influence they should rightly have."

Another fad of the sensitive sixties attempted to address the behavioral needs of effective organizations via structural mechanisms. Matrix management emerged from the showcase industry of the 1960s, aerospace, and specifically, from the star of the show, the space program. During its start-up years, NASA was faced with a seemingly overwhelming organizational task—how to mobilize thousands of talented experts, coordinate their efforts from plan through production, then quickly move them on to completely new tasks requiring new coordinating efforts, and so on. According to James Webb, original director of NASA, traditional bureaucratic structures were much too slow and too rigid for the complex tasks at hand. NASA hit upon increasing the flexibility and utilization of scarce resources by giving people dual responsibilities—functional and operational. A propulsion engineer, for example, would report vertically to the engineering manager and horizontally to a specific project manager. The crisscrossing lines of responsibility, when drawn on an organization chart, resulted in a matrix, hence the name "matrix management."

Variants of matrix management were quickly implemented by a host of high- and low-technology firms. Everyone from diaper manufacturers (Procter & Gamble) to dog food companies (Ralston Purina) to universities (Southern Methodist) was sold on the idea of the more fluid, flexible (and faddish) matrix form. Rarely, however, did the promised resource flexibility and utilization of matrix management come to pass. Two bosses more often made for confusion and competition than coordination, especially for the employee who was not only in the matrix but in the middle. Systems that were intended to be reflexive became redundant. Despite the glamorous success of the early NASA organization, most managers found the matrix quick fix to be not nearly so quick and not much of a fix.

Another decade of managerial fads drew to a close. By the late 1960s, managers were as disenchanted with sensitive, people-oriented fixes as they had been with the formula fixes of the 1950s. Moreover, there was a growing concern that the "touchy-feely" techniques and participative methods of the sixties had resulted in managers losing touch with costs, losing control of their businesses, and losing sight of their mission. The stage was set for the "strategic seventies."

One veteran of the sensitive sixties made this observation about the change in perspective the end of the decade brought. "After ten years of staring at our navels, we looked up and realized we were naked!" Businessmen were quick to clothe themselves in the traditional garb of cost control and profit maximization, which, this time around, bore such labels as zero-based budgeting, portfolio management, and the experience curve. This era of strategic analysis was also the heyday of the degree-granting MBA programs and high-priced MBAs.

Zero-based budgeting (ZBB) was a system of budget generation and review first popularized by Robert McNamara at Ford and later taken by him to the Defense Department. Traditionally, budgeting in most companies had amounted to little more than an exercise in addition, i.e., figure out how much was spent on an activity last year and add an increment for inflation to determine next year's level of expenditure. Rarely, if ever, did anyone ask, "Is this an activity we *ought* to be doing?" The idea of ZBB was to ask that question by reducing every line item to zero and building the budget up from that base through an inductive process: What is our goal? What results are expected? What activities do we need to do? With what resources? What alternatives are there? What is the threshold level of activity? What is essential? What more can be done at what cost? Why should it be done?

Presumably the ZBB process controlled costs by eliminating "automatic" budgetary increases and by making it possible to compare and therefore choose among alternative business activities. The logic of ZBB was very attractive to cost-conscious managers, and most major corporations adopted some form of the process. The operative word here is "form." In most corporations, it was the form, not the substance or even the philosophy, of ZBB that was implemented. Budgets were built in the language of ZBB—decision units, increments, threshold levels—and the forms were dutifully filled out. Meetings were held to make the tough priority decisions but these decisions typically turned on traditional issues of organizational politics, territory, and precedence. The result, after a complicated and often time-

18

consuming process, was that most companies ended up with budgets dictated largely by what was done last year.

In the seventies, corporations were not only looking at their budgets item by item; they were looking at their businesses, market by market. When the Mead Corporation contracted with the Boston Consulting Group in 1970, they collaborated on a concept of strategic planning that became one of the most pervasive management and marketing fads of the seventies. What came out of BCG was a perspective on multi-market businesses as a portfolio, each business in the portfolio demanding different management strategies. Using market share and market growth as yardsticks, the BCG analysis identified businesses as "stars," "cash cows," "question mark/new ventures," and "dogs," with attendant prescriptions for management. The *star* has both high market share and a rapidly growing market; the star has additional growth potential, and the profits are plowed back into the business in the form of investment for future growth. The *cash cow* is a mature business; it has a large market share but the market is no longer growing. Investment is no longer required, so the corporation receives a huge positive inflow of cash. The *question mark/ new venture* is a new business with high market-growth potential. In the initial stages, market share is low. When market share increases rapidly, the business is a prize heifer and will become a star; if market share stays low, it is a problem child. The *dog* is a poor performer with a small share of a stagnant and mature market. The dog typically adds little profit to the corporation and is often identified for sale to other corporations.[4]

Chesebrough-Pond's used the portfolio perspective with visible success in the early 1970s. Pond's Cold Cream and Vaseline Petroleum Jelly were the cash cows. Ragu Spaghetti Sauce, an unusual business for a health-care company, was acquired as a new venture and strategically managed into a "star." So, too, with Health-Tex, the children's clothing manufacturer. The strategy was repeated with the purchase of G. H. Bass shoemakers, then with Pond's own products, Rave home permanents and Prince Matchabelli men's fragrance.

So enchanted were managers with the portfolio prescriptions

for short-term action and long-range planning in the face of un-predictable futures that the strategic stereotyping of dogs, stars, cash cows, and question marks soon carried over into other aspects of business. Many companies began to characterize employees as deadwood, solid citizens, stars, and learners, based on their current performance and projected long-term potential.

The magic of portfolio management did not work wonders for all who tried it. Texas Instruments applied portfolio market analysis to its consumer products with disastrous results in the watch, calculator, and home computer businesses. General Electric treated consumer electronics as a cash cow, only to be taught by the Japanese that it is a star market where investment in research and development still has high payoffs. Other problems with portfolio management emerged as managers discovered that it was one thing to analyze one's portfolio and quite another to act on one's analysis—the effects on employee morale of labeling a business a cash cow or dog doomed many managers' master plans for their portfolios. Most companies' experience with portfolio management was intense but short-lived. During its short life-time, however, portfolio management did heighten the demand for MBAs, skilled at the types of analysis strategic management required.

In the early 1960s, MBAs were relatively rare. The country's three dozen or so MBA programs produced 5,000 MBAs per year. By the mid-1970s, there were over 500 degree-granting institutions churning out over 50,000 MBAs a year. Entry-level salaries soared to as much as $50,000 for MBAs from the right schools. Enrollments in MBA programs skyrocketed—not just full-time programs catering to inexperienced twenty-two- or twenty-three-year-olds but evening and part-time programs designed for those looking to improve their lot in organizational life; there were even weekend executive programs for senior managers looking for state-of-the-art skill updates.

Corporations soon were bursting at the seams with newly minted MBAs to man their newly adopted strategic planning programs, budget analysis divisions, and manpower planning systems. Whole departments were created to house these analysts. Staff assignments multiplied like hangers in a closet and so did salary expenses. One executive whose firm was caught up in the race for MBAs observed, "It seemed like every time we hired one, we had to hire two more so the first one would have someone to talk to. Then we had to put their boss in an executive MBA program so that he wouldn't feel inferior. Then the *real* managers, the ones who had responsibility for people and products, saw these number crunchers making huge salaries but making no direct contribution to the bottom line and so they demanded more money. Next thing you know we have twice as many people making twice as much money and we're not producing or selling one damn bit more than we were when we didn't know how to spell MBA!"

As systems and staffs proliferated, critics began to gang up on MBAs and on strategic analyses. Ultimately, the fad was hoisted on its own petard, exposed by cost/benefit analysis. More and more companies realized that after enormous resource investments in strategic planning systems and on the MBAs required to man them, productivity did not measurably improve nor did profitability. The benefits simply did not justify the costs. More embarrassing still, U.S. companies were falling further and further behind the Japanese and they didn't even have MBA programs in Japan! Could it be that the strategic perspective of the seventies had led managers too far afield? Hands-off, management-by-MBA hadn't delivered. Maybe hands-on, management-by-walking-around would. Welcome the "excellent eighties."

To chronicle all of the management fads of the eighties would require the space of several volumes. It has been a decade in which the search for the fix for all that ails business has been conducted with a fervor never before seen, impacting businesses from the boardroom to the shop floor and touching every employee and customer in the process. Even the most comprehensive listing of management magic of the last ten years is bound to be incomplete because it will neglect whatever has been hot since yesterday. Still, a few fads stand out.

In the early 1980s, American businessmen looked up from their portfolio classification models and PIMS (Profit impact of marketing strategies) analyses of profitability determinants and saw world markets dominated by the Japanese. From steel to skis, radars to radios, cars to computer chips—wherever the Japanese chose to compete, they built higher-quality products at lower prices. The market dominance of the Japanese all but negated the strategic planning efforts of American managers who, rather than managing their portfolios according to their strategic plans, were left to doing what the Japanese allowed them to do. Everyone wanted to know, "How do the Japanese do it?" The fixers had the answer.

The two books most identified with American business's rampant case of Japanophilia in the early eighties were William G. Ouchi's *Theory Z: How American Business Can Meet the Japanese Challenge* (1981) and *The Art of Japanese Management: Applications for American Executives* (1981), by Richard Tanner Pascale and Anthony G. Athos. Both books purported to describe how Japanese companies were managed, to explain why they were so successful, and to identify what American business executives could learn from the Japanese experience. The success of Japanese firms was attributed to such elements as lifetime employment, a generalist orientation, slow career progression, and collective decision making. To Ouchi, the single thing that made Japanese management distinctive was a clear articulation of the company purpose and philosophy throughout the organization. Theory Z organizations operate in this fashion, which is said to facilitate employee identification with and involvement in the enterprise. In Theory Z thinking, an involved worker is a productive worker. To American managers, the message was to get workers involved in the mission of the enterprise (it seemed quicker and easier than lifetime employment). The means to this end were quality circles: Groups of six to twelve employees from the same work area who typically meet once a week or on company time and on company premises to discuss and solve problems affecting their common work. They identify problems, analyze them, and then recommend solutions for quality and productivity improvements.

Once quality circles were "discovered" by Americans, they were everywhere. By one count in 1982, 44 percent of all companies with more than 500 employees had quality circle programs. The list included IBM, Xerox, Honeywell, Procter & Gamble, Westinghouse, Eastman Kodak, and thousands of smaller firms who followed in the footsteps of the corporate giants.

Quality circles were not the only management import from Japan. Athos and Pascale used McKinsey & Company's Seven S's to describe the success of Japanese firms. The Seven S's are strategy, structure, systems, staff, style, skills, and superordinate goals. American companies were said to be strong in the "hardball" S's—strategy, structure, and systems—but the Japanese were depicted as superior in the "soft" S's—staff, style, skills, and superordinate goals. More important, Japanese companies were presented as excelling in the complementary integration of all seven S's. In American companies, the different "S" elements were often seen to be in conflict. American managers, of course, took heed and ran amok looking after their S's.

Prideful American managers could take just so much of this America bashing. (Besides, it was proving to be damn difficult to get American workers to behave like Japanese.) Surely there were answers closer to home. They needed to look no further than the McKinsey & Company mirror. Two consultants from the "Big M," Tom Peters and Robert Waterman, looked at the firm's client list and saw eight common denominators in America's excellent companies: (1) bias for action; (2) staying close to the customer; (3) autonomy and entrepreneurship; (4) productivity through people; (5) hands-on, value-driven; (6) stick to the knitting; (7) simple form, lean staff; and (8) simultaneous loose-tight properties.[5] The list of excellent companies included over forty *Fortune* 500 firms, all generally regarded as the leaders in their respective fields. These eight characteristics of excellent organizations were like manna from heaven for hungry American managers. Excellence became an industry overnight, with record book sales, five-figure speaking fees, a television special, date books, T-shirts, hats—excellence quickly became the bellwether management fad of the eighties.

Critics suggested that excellence was oversimplified and trendy but managers saw little to criticize in the prescription for success and rushed to be excellent. When the popular business press began to point out the less-than-excellent performance of some of the excellent companies, even managerial proponents had to acknowledge that perhaps the emperor was naked. By the mid–1980s, most managers had grown weary of excellence. One West Coast bumper sticker proclaimed: "I'd rather be Dead than Excellent." Frustrated by prescriptions, managers were ready to hear that organizational success was more a product of the spirit or atmosphere of an organization than the result of specific prescribed elements. In the mid–1980s, the focus of managerial attention turned to "corporate culture," loosely translated as "the way we do things around here." The idea was that four dimensions of an organization created an aura or atmosphere that led workers to be productive, innovative, loyal, and so on. These four elements were (1) shared values; (2) rules, rites, and rituals; (3) heroes and legends; and (4) management practices. *Fortune* ran a feature article, "The Culture Vultures," chronicling corporate attempts to alter their ambiance. When EDS was purchased by General Motors, the culture clash between the two was as widely publicized as were the financial prospects. There was a story, no doubt apocryphal but widely circulated at the time, of the manager who, upon hearing a consultant's presentation on culture, turned to an aide and ordered, "That culture stuff sounds good. Let's have one in place by next week."

Of course, cultures evolve over long periods of time and are very complex, but that didn't stop the fixers from suggesting that management could change culture and, thereby, change behavior.

Although the fads of the 1980s emphasized overall organizational performance, the individual manager was not ignored. Witness Ken Blanchard and Spencer Johnson, whose *The One-Minute Manager* offered a simple prescription for managing using one-minute goal-setting, one-minute praising, one-minute reprimanding. Underlying their approach was a combination of management by objectives and behavior modification, but they made it so simple that it was immediately attractive to anyone who had been confounded by the experience of trying to manage the work of others. Vigorously promoted, and boasting a money-back guarantee, *The One-Minute Manager* was soon on virtually every desk in corporate America. CEOs ordered it purchased for everyone with management responsibility in everything from fried-chicken franchises to insurance companies. Managers bought it for themselves; employees bought it for their managers; working spouses gave it to each other. Everyone bought *The One-Minute Manager* but very few practiced it.

Why was something that was so popular, so logical, and so supremely simple so seldom practiced? One insurance executive captured the sentiments of many managers when he said, "The goals were damn hard to come up with; I couldn't possibly know every time my people did something right or wrong, and when it came right down to it, I felt a little foolish trying to let my people 'feel how I felt.' " Another manager said, "It worked fine on my kids, but one of my employees told me that at fifty-one years old he didn't need me trying to be his goddamn daddy!" As the 1980s waned, managers learned that people deserved and demanded much more than one minute of their time. Simple solutions were unlikely to solve even the simplest of problems.

Theory Z, excellence, corporate culture, and the one-minute manager represent only the most well known of the management fads and fixes of the eighties. Intrapreneuring, downsizing, networking, just-in-time manufacturing, visionary leadership, and a host of other instant answers all had periods of popularity during the decade, which has been a time of unprecedented promotion of management panaceas. But despite the quantity of executive elixirs in the eighties, qualitatively they differ not at all from the kind of advice given forty years ago. Indeed, there is something to be learned from the predictable cycle of management fads.

For over forty years, the fads and fixes that have attracted managers and their organizations have followed a predictable cycle. The excellence fad of the eighties came and went in much the same fashion as PERT/CPM did in the 1950s, even as scientific management did a half a century before.

Every quick fix has worked for someone, somewhere, sometime. The larger, more visible the company, the more likely it is that the particular management program or technique to which the company attributes its success will be copied by others and thus begin the fad cycle.

When General Electric decentralized operations in 1950, thousands of companies rushed to follow suit. The putative success of the Managerial Grid at companies such as Lever Brothers Limited, Humble Oil, and Bell Telephone spawned Grid seminars in organizations throughout the private and public sector in the sixties. Mead Corporation credited its success in the seventies to the strategic planning models of the Boston Consulting Group, resulting in whole new organization units and careers in the organizations that rushed to copy Mead. The reputation alone of Peters and Waterman's excellent companies was enough to encourage others to emulate whatever it was those celebrity corporations were doing to make them excellent.

It is not enough that a fix be successful for it to become a fad. It must be successful in a sizable company. There are thousands of small companies who are successful in a million small ways, but their successes will, in all likelihood, never be imitated because they are never seen. It is more than "out of sight, out of mind." There is in the mind of managers a belief that the big companies do it best. In management, fads start in the *Fortune* 500.

The next step in the cycle of a fad is capturing the "simple truth" that is the key to success. Acronymic formulas and numeric steps are the acme of reductionism here—MBO, PERT,

9–9 management, seven S's, eight dimensions of excellence, one-minute managing; the list goes on. There appear to be some guiding rules. Acronyms must be five letters or less and preferably spell something. When Paul Hersey and Ken Blanchard first developed their leadership seminar, it was based on the Leader Adaptability and Style Inventory. Unfortunately, the resulting acronym—LASI—did not suggest a dynamic model of management. They subsequently changed the instrument to Leader Effectiveness and Adaptability Description—LEAD.

The required numerical steps for a quick fix ought not to exceed single digits; three, four, seven, and eight seem most popular. Hand in hand with the simplicity of the solution is the speed with which it can be implemented—after all, this is to be a *quick fix*. Clearly, *The One-Minute Manager* is the ideal here.

Whatever the acronym or numbered steps, the simple truth of the solution, if it is to take on fad status, should convey the sense that it is true *because* it is simple. There is something inherently attractive about simple solutions regardless of the complexity of the issue confronting managers. Perhaps it appeals to the anti-science bias of managers. It is almost as though anything that cannot be reduced to simple truths cannot work. Certainly it cannot succeed as a fad.

If there is one way in which the management quick fixes of today are dramatically different from their forebears of forty years ago, it is the way they are sold. In the fifties, fixes were passed from one company to another by word of mouth and via transient executives. In the sixties and early seventies, consultants became the principal purveyors of panaceas. Still, these salesmen hawked their wares largely behind closed corporate doors. Today, management quick fixes are mass-marketed, prepackaged, and promoted like mouthwash or McNuggets.

The formula for a fix in the eighties requires a best-selling book, videotapes, audiocassette programs with workbooks, a star-turn lecture series, seminars, and assorted paraphernalia, gimme-caps, T-shirts, etc. There is truly a "quick fix" industry and each fix is a product with attendant market strategy, add-ons and spin-offs, and franchisees. There seems to be an attitude among managers that if the message isn't packaged for mass marketing, it can't be worth very much.

A history professor tells of the time he was invited by a businessmen's association to give a luncheon talk on business leadership fifty years ago versus business leadership today. An accomplished speaker, he captivated the group and they responded with many questions until one of the members asked if he had "copies of his book they could buy, or perhaps some tape cassettes?" He had to admit that he had written no book, produced no cassettes, whereupon his audience proceeded to ignore him. He encapsulates the experience with the observation, "I had them in the palm of my hand until they realized I didn't have T-shirts to sell." Franchising the fix, with all of the accoutrements, is an integral part in the cycle of a management fad. Today, franchising the fix is necessary to position a management fad to become a social phenomenon.

Not all quick fixes become fads. Many lack the required sizable success or simple truth or franchising that makes for being "in" with managers. For those fixes that do become fads, the next evolution is to become so "in" that anyone who is not doing it is, by definition, "out." At this point, the fad is a phenomenon.

In the 1970s, mid-careerists returned to school to get their MBAs not so much for the knowledge provided as to keep up with the competition, the incoming MBAs. In the 1980s, the best-selling pop-management books were required reading in most business schools not for their intrinsic value but for their extrinsic value. It was presumed that they were on every executive's desk and, therefore, were required reading for would-be executives. So as it has been with each of the major management fads, it becomes a phenomenon at that point when it is done not simply because it is the thing to do but because there is something wrong if you're not doing it. The phenomenon stage brings a fad to the threshold of fading out.

When, in November 1984, *Business Week* highlighted the poor performances of some of the "excellent companies," it was final testimony that excellence had run its course among managers. Management fads are always viewed with cynicism by business school professors, *Wall Street Journal* reporters, and other detached, presumably objective observers of managerial maneuverings. Attacks from these quarters on the simplicity and surety of ostensible solutions come early in the life of a quick fix. If these attacks are seen or heard at all, they are just as quickly dismissed by managers, who, for the most part, are of the opinion that they have little to learn from academics when it comes to managing. As the fix gains momentum and takes on fad status, more managers employ it, and more find it wanting. Anecdotal reports of the shortcomings begin to be passed from manager to manager. Still, everyone seems to be doing it. Once everyone actually is doing it, the evidence is overwhelming. Experience with the fix is, at this point, widespread enough to provide real tests that are readily observable. Under this sort of scrutiny, every management phenomenon is likely to be found wanting. When business publications take up the attack, the fad is fading out. (Rarely do these publications acknowledge their own estimable role in promoting the fixes at their onset.)

No sooner had *Business Week* attacked "excellence" than Peters was back with *A Passion for Excellence*, or "Son of Search," as some pundits referred to it. Critics of the impracticality of *The One-Minute Manager* were answered in *Putting the One-Minute Manager to Work*. *Theory Z* gave way to *The M-Form Society*. And so it goes and has always gone.

Promoters have always found in the flaws of their fixes the seeds of sequels. Usually these sequels find an audience only among the truly committed, those not yet disenchanted with the fix or discouraged by its critics. Most management faddists are much too fickle to give sequels a second glance; they've already moved on to the next new thing and have little regard for recycled revelations. As soon as the sequel is available, the fad, no matter how "in" it was, is out—out of fashion and into the corporate closet.

The bookshelves, file cabinets, storage closets, and, in some instances, warehouses of corporate America are full of the flotsam and jetsam of former fixes. Books, workbooks, charts, plaques, certificates, audiocassettes, videotapes—it's all there, magical ministrations and grand designs now gathering dust. In many companies, scanning executive bookshelves is like touring a museum of management fads or, as one manager expressed it more inelegantly: "It's our sure-thing scrap heap. Really, we've got this large walk-in closet where all that stuff ends up. Now that we're into cost-cutting, we are finally getting some payoff out of all those programs we bought over the years. We're copying over the tapes, using the notebooks for our presentations, drawing on the backside of charts—it's saving us a lot of money."

Few companies go to this extreme to get value from their fix investment. Indeed, many are embarrassed by the remains of their excesses. Questions are quickly brushed aside: "What are those tapes?" "Were those notebooks part of some company program?" "Where did you get that hat?" The common answer is, "Oh, that's just left over from something we did for a while. It's not important now."

"It's not important now." Nothing could more adequately summarize the cycle of a management fad. Whether in the fifties or in the future, it is the very nature of a quick fix that it will be "something we did for a while. It's not important now." Why, in the face of forty years of experience with fixes, in the face of evidence of a predictable cycle to management fads, in the face of few (if any) lasting effects, do managers continue to be attracted to the quick fix?

The size and scope of the management fad industry today has prompted many to try to explain the fascination with fixes. Peter Drucker thinks that the love of panaceas is not new, nor is it exclusively managerial; rather, it is endemic: "It's an old habit. We love panaceas, the quick fix which can solve everything from bad breath to cancer. It has always been in the forefront of American politics because panaceas are dynamic. Many groups can instantly organize around them. It has been the same in medicine. Modern medicine began when it stopped looking for one universal cure and looked, instead, for specific cures for specific ailments. One always pays the price for quick fixes."

Many cultural observers would agree; they see an inherent, perennial attraction in simple solutions that is heightened by the increasing complexity of the world. A vice-president of Levi Strauss framed the management quick-fix popularity succinctly, observing, "The books may be a source of interest to business students in the future because they so poignantly reflect the insecurity of the business environment of the early 1980s."

The human habit of looking for the quick and easy way, the added allure of self-managed simplicity in a complex world, and managerial insecurity underlie the unprecedented managerial interest in quick fixes. One author has described this contemporary phenomenon as the Panacean Conspiracy: "These managers, typically promoted into management from such technical specialties as engineering, law, or finance, have little managerial knowhow. Most don't have the time, interest, or awareness needed to learn their new craft, but they are anxious to produce immediately. What they are looking for, although they may profess to know better, are quick-fix solutions to dynamic, complex problems."[6]

There is yet another factor that contributes to managers' fixation with quick fixes that deserves mention—the failure of science.

Management today is more complex and more dynamic than ever before. These conditions translate into greater risks and, therefore, greater pressures. Given the circumstances faced by modern executives, their search for effective new ideas is understandable. The time seems right for a cooperative inquiry between science and industry into the problems that have priority to managers and the solutions that look promising to academics. In fact, this has not happened. If anything, there is an antiscience, anti-intellectual sentiment among managers today. In part, this is because the very processes of science—the deliberate (slow) search for specific (not universal) alternatives (not solutions) to

31

be administered by experts (not managers) in complex (not simple) situations—flies in the face of what managers want.

It may be that managers have been too easily enticed by the easy formulas of the fixers. It may also be that they have had nowhere else to turn in their search for new approaches. Certainly science has had little to offer managers in a form that they could use. Indeed, it could be said that the management sciences have been decidedly antimanagement. Consider the titles of these recent articles from some of the top management journals: "An Approach for Confirmatory Measurement and Structural Equation Modeling of Organizational Properties," *Management Science;* "The Administrative Component of Organizations and the Ratchet Effect: A Critique of Cross-Sectional Studies," *Journal of Management Studies;* "A Comparison of Multiple Constituency Models of Organizational Effectiveness," *Academy of Management Review.* A busy executive facing escalating pressures to perform in an increasingly complex business environment can hardly be faulted for choosing to read popular management manuals over what is available to him in the management journals. Business school professors ridicule the "corporate summer camps" and self-help seminars promoted by itinerant management consultants, but what do they offer in their place? A recent public seminar at a university near Dallas was on "Nomothetic Versus Idiographic Orientations in Research on Organizations." The sponsors expressed dismay that no one from the business community attended.

John W. Slocum, former president of the Academy of Management, in his presidential address to the membership in 1984 catalogued the differences between the problems of managers and the pursuits of management scholars. He concluded with this chastisement: "It seems management scholars have traded off solving smaller or trivial problems well, instead of larger ones. It's what we call 'the error of the Third Kind,' solving the wrong problem well." Professor Slocum is on target; there is no doubt that the academy has abandoned management at the very time when management is most in need of help from any and every quarter.

Habitual human cravings for quick and easy answers, the seductive allure of simple solutions in a complex world, and the failure/neglect of science all explain why modern managers have cast their lot with the sellers of salvation. Who's to say that they haven't chosen correctly? What's the harm in looking for help wherever you can find it? What's bad about fads?

It is very popular today to find fault with management fads, with those who purvey fads and with those who purchase them. The quick-fix industry has spawned an antifix press. With the perfect vision that hindsight and ivory towers provide, the flaws in fixes are easily spotlighted, the fix mentality reviled as marginally moronic. In this rush to criticize, the positive contributions of fixes are frequently overlooked.

It cannot be denied that management fads can spur experimentation, innovation, and change, all important considerations for organizations in dynamic environments. Alfred J. Battaglia, president of Becton Dickinson Vascutainer Systems, correctly observes that it's "okay to criticize gimmickry, but let's not stop experimenting. If we do, we may stop learning." The caveat here is that there is a difference between viewing management fads as experiments and viewing them as proven solutions. The former perspective does lead to learning, the latter leads to unexamined imitation.

Management fads can focus attention on neglected dynamics in the organization, catalyze thinking about old habits in new ways, and generally energize people. A sales executive observed, "When a company gets into a fad, it's like a big sales promotion. Everyone gets excited, it gets the adrenaline pumping and a lot of good things can happen. Of course, sustaining that attitude is another story."

To be fair, there are some sustaining elements that come from management fads; they are not all as frivolous and fleeting as they would seem. Some of the instant cures embody sound ideas, though they may promise more than they can possibly deliver. "You can go back to management-by-objective, son of management-by-objective, management-by-objective meets appraisal-and-counseling," says E. Kirby Warren, professor at Columbia

University's Graduate School of Business. "Most of these fads would have some real value if senior management took the time to ask themselves: (1) How do I adapt the idea to our culture and business? (2) What has to be changed to reinforce the thing we're talking about? (3) Are we committed to staying with it long enough to make it work?"

Many companies have culled from the popular cures those elements they believe to be most effective. These elements have been woven into the fabric of ongoing organizational practices in many successful companies. Dale D. McConkey, long a defender of MBO, writes that the reason we don't hear much of MBO today is because it has been successful: "True, we don't hear the term used as frequently as we used to. However, this is a tribute to MBO's effectiveness and the extensive degree to which it has been adopted. Because most successful organizations have been practicing it for so long, it has been woven into the corporate cloth." Defenders of fads are quick to point out that everything that is now standard operating procedure in organizations was once viewed as a fad.

Setting aside for the moment the question of whether or not quick fixes do (or ever *could*) live up to their promotional claims, it is true that management fads can (1) serve to catalyze change, (2) energize people and organizations, (3) embody sound ideas, and (4) become an effective part of organizations' standard operating procedures. So what's wrong with fixes and fads?

Morphine is one of many drugs that has beneficial effects in certain limited circumstances but which, in the main, should be avoided because it is highly addictive and ultimately destructive. Fads and fixes should be viewed in the same way. True, there are some very specific circumstances in which a popular panacea may be just the cure for a lethargic organization, but as a rule, the proven costs far outweigh the potential benefits.

At the outset, we need to talk costs—economic costs and opportunity costs. Fads and fixes (like any prescription medicine these days) are expensive. Books, videos, audiocassettes, workbooks, buttons, and the other paraphernalia of panaceas are costly to produce. Off-site retreats and seminars, often held at resort locations, are additional expense items. Add to this consultants' fees: companies pay up to $15,000 a day to sit at the feet of the most popular fixers; even your corner consultant is likely to charge $1,000 to $1,500 a day (and he's never been on a talk show).

As alarming as these figures are, they are only the monetary costs of management fads. If one were to factor in the opportunity costs, those costs incurred by executives, managers, and employees spending time on activities other than their jobs, the expense of fad management becomes truly staggering. Seminars, workshops, rallies, group meetings, and other assorted "training" activities, which are the means to most management fixes, can consume massive amounts of man-hours. Moreover, the things that go on in these activities rarely transfer readily to the job. Fixes then can be doubly costly to the firm, taking time away from jobs and taking time to teach skills that may be only remotely job-related.

The other significant cost associated with fads and fixes is the cost to corporate credibility. When companies invest heavily in the fad approach, employees see management as abdicating their responsibility for the management of the enterprise to a "high priest of hype." The message sent by management is that all that is needed is to hire a consultant, plug in a new program, and presto, the company will be innovative, productive, excellent. Stanley Bing, business columnist for *Esquire*, has these observations on living in a fad culture: "You'll have to excuse us guys on the inside if we get a little giggly each time the next new dogma comes along. We've been converted before, after all. We've managed in a minute and Theory Z'd, spotted megatrends, spun matrices, woven grids; we've hammered ourselves into hard-networking Intrapreneurs, sat in stupefaction before lanky preachers nagging us to *Be Excellent!* Some of us, thank God, have even found Wellness. We're willing to give each new creed a chance, until its hasty priests begin torturing the innocent into false confessions."[7]

Employees know firsthand the complexities of organization life. The simple solutions embodied in faddish fixes are typically seen by employees as little more than Band-Aids for what are systemic illnesses. Moreover, employees have to live with the consequences of applying one Band-Aid after another. As one veteran supervisor observed, "Band-Aids are great for cuts and scratches, but they don't do much for cancer. What we have in this plant is cancer. I'm afraid it may be terminal."

When employees lose faith in the acumen and actions of management, no fad or fix, regardless of how popular, can remedy the situation. The cost of a loss of credibility, which so often is a consequence of fad management, is a cost that cannot be easily recouped.

There is yet another cost of fads and fixes, so large that it dwarfs the direct and indirect expense of fad management, so lasting it undermines even the most credible of managers. *It is the cost of believing in the myths of modern management.*

Today's business environment is more complex and dynamic than any experienced heretofore. Changing markets, changing technology, and a changing work force demand that managers be both analytical and adaptive. With these changes and challenges come tremendous opportunities to create new products and new processes to manage the future. So long as managers seek the quick fix, so long as they manage by fad, these opportunities will be wasted. To create the future for their organizations, managers must have a grasp on the present. The myths of management distort reality, they promote habitual means and ends, they hobble imagination. The challenge in the changes and complexity of today's business environment is to set aside the habits and constraints fostered by fads and fixes, to ground oneself in the reality of today's management problems and, from that reality, to reach for the future. The challenge is to *manage without the myths.*

For managers to discard the myths that distort managerial reality and respond creatively to managing the future, they need to understand the myths regarding megafirms, entrepreneurial management, leadership, motivation, MBAs, and technology. Understanding these myths requires more than knowing what they are; it requires knowing how they are used and what they mean. Discovery of the future requires uncovering the present and revealing one's own involvement in the myths that constrain oneself. In order to manage the future, managers must free themselves of the fads and fixes—the modern myths. Managing without myths means that managers must be introspective, willing to look at themselves, at their own behavior, at their own myths—in short, managers must be willing to learn from their own experiences. This book is about those experiences and what can be learned from them.

3

The Myth of the Megafirm

We don't manage by managing. We manage by being there all the time.
—Chuck Sussman,
President, Pretty Neat Industries, Inc.

In 1953, Charles E. Wilson, then president of General Motors, was nominated by President Eisenhower to be secretary of defense. During the Senate confirmation hearings, Wilson was asked if he would be willing as secretary, if necessary, to make a decision unfavorable to General Motors. "Engine Charlie" responded, "What's good for the country is good for General Motors, and vice versa."

Twenty-six years later, in September 1979, Chrysler Corporation, the fourteenth largest industrial firm in America, was near bankruptcy. Lee Iacocca, president of Chrysler, appeared before the Senate Banking Committee to petition the federal government for financial help. He argued that Chrysler was too big to fail; there were too many employees; there were too many stockholders; there were too many small business suppliers. In short, Iacocca argued that the size of Chrysler ordained that the company be saved *for the country*. Borrowing the logic of Engine Charlie, Iacocca told the senators, "My problems are the problems of the country."

In the minds of corporate presidents and the country's politicians, the fortunes of America have always been tied to big business. Even business historians have declared that "the large business corporation is *the* distinguishing feature of the structure of American industry and the American economy."[1] Business, government, and academe have led the public at large to picture the business of America as *big* business. What we know about business today comes largely from studies of big businesses and the men and women who have been successful in them. So pervasive is this perception that "big business" has become personified, we speak and write of "big business" as though it had a single, identifiable mind and spirit. When Americans think business, we think big.

Megafirm corporate America is one of the most pervasive and perfidious myths of modern management. The large business corporation may be the distinguishing feature of the American economy, but it is far from the most descriptive. The vast majority of us own, manage, or work in *small* businesses, workplaces where there are fewer than one hundred employees. Corporate takeovers, multinational agreements, board politics, seven-figure financing, and six-figure salaries may be the stuff of best-sellers and soap operas but are foreign to business as most of us know it—small, personal, even familial. The myth of the megafirm misleads managers into thinking that the lessons learned in corporate corridors apply with equal effectiveness to the closets and cubbyholes that are more commonly our workplaces. The truth of modern management is that most of what we know about megafirms has little to do with work and management as we know it. It is a small-business world, and a small business is not a little big business.

Corporate takeovers are headline stories, CEOs star as cover boys for popular magazines, and boardroom maneuverings provide story lines for TV's prime-time dramas. Lost to most amid the glitz and glamour surrounding megafirms is a government report that presents a very different picture of American business. *The State of Small Business: A Report of the President Transmitted to the Congress, March 1984* shows the business of

America to be small business. Developments in the ensuing years have only reinforced this finding; the facts are quite revealing.

Measured by asset size alone, the economy is dominated by small businesses. Corporations with assets of less than $1 million account for 91.4 percent of all corporations. When corporations in the $1-million-to-$10-million-asset range are included, 98.7 percent of *all* corporations are accounted for. The megafirms, those with assets of over $100 million, constitute less than .2 percent of America's corporate mix. Since 1970, companies with assets of less than $1 million have nearly doubled (93.6 percent). There is overwhelming evidence that small companies are the economic base of America.

The Small Business Administration defines small businesses as those with fewer than 500 employees. There are roughly 15 million businesses in the United States, and 98 percent qualify as small businesses. For every one business with over 100 employees, there are forty-six businesses with under twenty employees. Almost 80 percent of America's small businesses have between one and nineteen employees—including the owner and his or her family. These small businesses employ over 55 percent of the private work force, account for nearly 45 percent of all sales, and make up 43 percent of the gross national product.

Over the last ten years, the trend in American business has been increasingly toward smaller enterprises. Since 1975, the *Fortune* 500 companies have decreased employment, yet nationwide there has been a net increase in the number of jobs. Small businesses are creating the new jobs in America. One extensive study reported that nearly 75 percent of new private-sector jobs were created by firms of fifty employees or fewer and 47 percent by firms of twenty or fewer. The small-business boom has actually been fueled in part by layoffs and cutbacks in the megafirms as many people have come to realize that corporate tenure is not necessarily secure.

Much of the job growth in small businesses is driven by the high-technology and service industries, which offer readily accessible entrepreneurial opportunities. In recent years, the greatest job growth has come from four areas: computers and data processing; hotels, motels, and restaurants; audiovisual sales and service; and amusement and recreation services.

Nowadays, it seems as though everyone knows someone who started part-time in the garage or spare room and made it big almost overnight in one of these areas. The small businessman, the entrepreneur, has become something of a culture hero.

Fast-track, high-tech entrepreneurs may be the glamour side of the small-business boom, but most small businesses are far from glamorous. In fact, most fail. Two out of ten small businesses don't make it to their first anniversary, eight out of ten are defunct within ten years. The highest failure rate is found in small, miscellaneous retailers—today's boutique equivalent of mom-and-pop operations—hobby, book, gift, sporting-goods stores, and florists. The most successful small businesses are the least glamorous of all—fewer than 1 percent of funeral homes go under. One of America's oldest companies, Kirk and Nice Inc., which built coffins for the American and British soldiers who fell at the Battle of Germantown in 1777, still conducts over five hundred funerals a year in Philadelphia under the eighth generation of family management. Other good-risk small businesses are tobacco wholesalers, laundries, and drugstores. These small businesses are not the glamorous go-go firms; they are more accurately characterized as low and slow—low technology, slow growth. In these, as in most successful small businesses, there is more grit than glamour; twenty-four-hour days come long before twenty-four-karat Rolexes, and positive cash flow is far more important than corporate culture.

This is the business of America. It is business as most of us know it, far removed from the megafirms that spawn the management fads and fixes. It is folly to think that the successful management techniques of the megafirms can contribute much to those who work in small businesses, who have precious little time and resources for megafirm concerns such as strategic planning, corporate culture, mergers, and management magic. For most of us, ours is a work world of long hours, negative cash flow, and people problems with customers and coworkers whom we care about. Ours is a small-business world. It is our *real* world and it is worlds removed from the management myth of the mega-firm.

John Welsh and Jerry White are professors at Southern Methodist University who study and advise small businesses. Their landmark article, "A Small Business Is Not a Little Big Business," captures the myth of the megafirm succinctly: "A traditional assumption among managers has been that small businesses should use essentially the same management principles as big businesses, only on a smaller scale. Underlying that assumption has been the notion that small companies are much like big companies, except that small businesses have lower sales, smaller assets, and fewer employees."[2]

The truth is, a small business is *not* a little big business and the differences have an important message for managers. Welsh and White argue convincingly that the very size of small businesses creates special conditions that distinguish them from their larger counterparts. These distinguishing characteristics, in turn, require some very different management approaches. A small business is not a little big business because of (1) time and money, (2) products and processes, and (3) people.

Chuck Sussman, the famous and, at times, infamous mail-order entrepreneur of "man-made diamonds" and miracle odor removers, has reflected on the critical role cash plays in the small business: "In a big company, they do projections. They say, 'In the first quarter, we're going to lose so many million; in the second quarter, we're going to lose so many; and by year two, we're going to be profitable.' With the little guy, if you don't make money the first week, you're out of business. You've got to be making money now!"

The small business's need to "make money now" reflects the condition Welsh and White refer to as resource poverty. Small businesses tend to be clustered in highly fragmented industries with many competitors; instant copy shops, dry cleaners, restaurants, video rental stores, and the like are common examples. In these industries, businesses must often cut prices to the bone in order to increase market share and raise revenues. Low margins and low volume result in low revenues and resource poverty for small businesses.

The ability of small businesses to borrow resources is severely limited. The credit needs of small businesses are largely for working capital. With few tangible assets to borrow against, small businesses are typically seriously undercapitalized. A commonly heard complaint among failed small businessmen is that they underestimated the time and money required for start-up. One restaurateur lamented, "Six months more and we would have made it, but with nothing to borrow against, I had no prayer of getting six months' more financing."

External forces—changes in government regulations, tax laws, labor, and interest rates—affect a greater percentage of expenses for small businesses than they do for large corporations. Small businesses are more vulnerable to outside economic pressures because they have little time and/or money available to manage their environment, e.g., get favorable legislation passed.

Small businesses are more vulnerable to internal economic forces as well. The owner-manager's salary in a small business represents a larger fraction of revenues than in a big company. Not only is there little left over to pay additional managers or reward investors, but the company finances are inextricably linked to the owner-manager's finances and his or her ability to raise capital.

The economic realities surrounding small businesses are underscored by Bill McGowan, who shaped MCI into a communications megafirm. Commenting on what he learned from his prior experience as a management consultant specializing in failing small companies, he said: "Small companies, private companies, especially, should ignore the accountants' profit-and-loss statements. They are a snare and a trap; they force you after the wrong thing. The only thing that matters is cash flow—not the cash flows they use today, but the old cash flows that laid out the source and application of funds—where it's coming from and where it's going and how much is left over."[3]

The resource poverty that small businesses live with every day is a condition that most of us dealing with family budgets can easily relate to. Resource poverty is a condition completely foreign to megafirms, which live by the old financial adage, "Borrow a little money and you have a creditor, borrow a lot of money and you have a partner, borrow enough money and you have an underwriter." For example, the drop in oil prices in 1985 and 1986 made partners of many oil companies and their banks, who had so much money in the oil patch that they could not call in the loans for fear of defaults.

The financial structure of megafirms is such that they can afford to think of down-quarters and long-term projections. Financial fat smooths short-term fluctuations for large businesses, evens out the impact of seasonal variations in sales, and helps overcome one-time calamitous events. Deep pockets enabled Johnson & Johnson to survive the Tylenol scare, Union Carbide to recoup from the Bhopal incident, and Delta Airlines to deal with the 1985 Dallas crash of Flight 191. On the financial statements, the result of such catastrophes is normally smaller rates of change in annual growth. In the minds of megafirm managers and employees, substantial financial resources can lead to an illusion of perpetuity. Everyone learns that the appropriate perspective is long-term and large-scale, and decisions are made accordingly.

Deep financial pockets mean that megafirms can minimize risks significantly. Having both the resources and the time to overcome mistakes greatly reduces the risks entailed by exploring a quick fix, the effects of which may be ephemeral. The management tactics and techniques that emerge from this megafirm mentality are grandiose in scale and often cavalier with regard to costs, understandably so, as time and money are in apparently abundant supply in megafirms. Nowhere is this mentality more evident than in "strategic planning."

The purpose of strategic planning is to help a company achieve its goals and, in the process, to develop a sustainable advantage over its competitors. Strategic planning is based on an ends-ways-means model. Corporate objectives (ends) are established, strategies (ways) developed for attaining them, and then the necessary resources (means) marshaled. These strategic plans are based typically on five- to- ten-year time frames. This promotes a top-down "strategic leap" mentality in an organization, literally leaping forward to envision the company as it might be five or ten years into the future. These leaps can take a variety of forms: product redesign, factory modernization or expansion, a relocation, acquisition of a supplier of a critical material or component, or adopting a new technology.

As Professor Robert H. Hayes of the Harvard Business School has observed, these strategies for developing strategy have significant corporate implications: "Such big steps are highly visible and usually require a major expenditure of funds. Therefore, much staff development is required, and the expertise of many highly specialized people—financial analysts, strategic planners, legal experts, and outside consultants—must be tapped. In such companies, the corporate staff is regarded as the elite, and assignments of line managers to staff positions are typically felt to be promotions. This strategy does not require outstanding, highly trained people at lower levels in the organization. Their job is simply to operate the structure that top management and its staff of experts have created."[4]

A corollary to Hayes's observations is that in addition to the requirements for staff, strategic planning systems require significant financial wherewithal—both to develop and implement strategy, and to sustain the enterprise for the five or ten years required for strategic plans to come to fruition. Megafirms certainly have the time and money for strategic planning, but it is pure myth to imagine that any but the largest, most secure of corporations can afford this luxury. Most of us work in circumstances much closer to the resource poverty that characterizes small businesses. There is no time to defer, no time to develop; there is only time to *do* and only today's time and money to do it with.

The availability of time and money cannot help but have an impact upon performance. The relative resource poverty afflicting small businesses is manifest in the way they go about doing

45

what they do. This does not mean that small businesses do not produce quality goods and services equal to those of larger competitors. Nor does it suggest that small-business management methods and techniques are less effective or efficient than those of the megafirms. In fact, there is considerable evidence to suggest that smaller businesses have quality and efficiency advantages over megafirms. But there is no denying that the methods of small businesses are *very* different from those of the megafirms.

Thomas P. Murphy, who writes a column on venture capital for *Forbes*, tells of one encounter between a megafirm-trained executive and his entrepreneur boss: "The new executive, with staff work worthy of the German Army, had concluded that a $100,000 stainless-steel mold for making plastic extrusions was a far better long-run investment than a $10,000 aluminum mold that wouldn't last as long. Indeed, it was true. There was only one thing wrong with the analysis: the business did not have $100,000. It was, in fact, almost broke. The entrepreneur patiently explained to his new executive that he was more concerned with staying alive over the short term than with which mold was best in the long run."

The size and resource vulnerability of small businesses mean that they must do things differently than their megafirm competitors. This often means doing things better; small businesses can—indeed *must*—be more creative, more flexible. Jim Schroth, founder of J. L. Schroth, Michigan manufacturers of rubber parts for automobiles, describes how his company responded to a request from Ford Motor Company: "I got a call on a Wednesday from an engineer at Ford who needed a little part shaped like a strawberry. I got the company next door, which does prototype stamping, to make part of the thing up. My toolmaker put all the people he needed on it, and I delivered the parts to Ford on Friday. It would have taken them weeks."

Larry Stanley, owner of Empire Bolt and Screw Company in Spokane, Washington, says the responsiveness demonstrated by Schroth is the major advantage of small business. "It [big business] has the same lack of flexibility, poor communications, and slowness of response as government." Mr. Stanley deals regularly with megafirms such as Textron, ITT, Bethlehem Steel, and 3M. Such big suppliers, he adds, have difficulty shipping his orders in less than three days. "No small supplier takes longer than twenty-four hours."

Dale Jahr, senior economist for the Joint Economic Committee of Congress, suggests the large corporations may no longer have the competitive edge. "In a dynamic and high-tech economy, 'bigness' may be an impediment to adapting to rapidly changing business conditions. Liquidity and mobility are the modern advantages; massive amounts of sedentary capital tend to rust or rot. While economies of scale exist in manufacturing, natural resources and public utilities, the same might not be true for emerging industries of the information age."[5]

The competitive advantage of small businesses lies in the greater creativity and innovation in their products and processes. The obverse side—lack of stability, lack of predictability—is the competitive disadvantage. As one purchasing agent for a defense contractor observed, "The guy operating out of a garage down the street may be able to get ten of what you need to you by tomorrow but can he get ten thousand to you next month and every month after that for the length of your contract? Can he make good on a defective shipment? Can he support what he sells? I'm much more concerned about the capacity and the control of my suppliers than I am their creativity."

Questions of capacity and control strike at the Achilles' heel of small businesses. The sophisticated tools of management, such as strategic planning, are usually not available because of the time and money requirements. Sid Atkinson, managing director of the entrepreneurial firm Living Quarters, misses the corporate capacity to plan: "One thing I do miss is being able to make any long-term management plans. In a small business, you have to be a lot more earthbound. In fact, business has turned out to be more mundane than I expected; the enjoyment of planning is often negated by time-consuming, routine activities."

Differences between the processes of megafirms and those of small businesses may be most evident to outsiders in their approaches to marketing. The small business cannot afford market surveys, consumer research, or salary surveys. There are no four-color sales brochures, no sales support staff, no research or financial analysts, no public relations office, and no print shop. Cliff Evans, president of the Henderson Corporation, a Raritan, New Jersey, construction company, describes what happens when he goes head to head against the conglomerate competition: "We used to give a potential client a list of past clients, tell him to pick three at random and call them. That system doesn't always sell the job anymore. The biggies bring in a dog and pony show, with sound effects and visual aids, and they dazzle clients." The megafirms have staffs of dazzlers; in small businesses the deal-makers, the doers, the dazzlers, and the dustman are usually all one and the same.

In the absence of staffs—marketing, financial planning, or whatever—admonitions from the megafirm fixers toward "lean staff" or "staying close to the customer" strike small-business operators as nothing more than frivolous sloganeering. There is *no* staff, therefore no question of fat or lean. Bob Bushansky, owner of Royal Industrial Supply Company, a $3-million-a-year janitorial supply firm, says, "I meet these guys from corporations and I start telling them about my problems. They say, 'Let your staff take care of that.' They don't understand. There is no staff."

The absence of staff is only one management support service small businessmen must do without. Frank Peters, who along with four colleagues left a large corporation to start up a small manufacturing concern, reflects on some of the differences he's experienced. "There are things I always regret giving up—like big, fast Xerox machines, the speed with which the personnel department can replace a secretary, and the quality of the company car. When all those support services you were used to in a big company now cost you money, you learn to do without. While the cost of supplying senior staff with relatively expensive cars scarcely shows in a large company, it is very important in a small outfit." Peters, like most small businessmen, has an intimate knowledge of where the costs are in his company; in order to survive, he has to stay close to his costs.

The owner/operator doesn't have to worry about staying close to the customer either; as his company's number-one (often *only*) salesperson and provider of sales/service/support, he is with the customer constantly—in the showroom, on the shop floor, in the kitchen, or behind the cash register. He has to be. In a small business, there is such a fine line between success and failure that the slightest neglect or oversight can wipe out today's profits and tomorrow's inventory. Moreover, absent any technological advantage, it may be that the constant presence of the owner/operator and the resulting service "from the top" is the one small business advantage that the megafirms cannot match.

Much of management in the megafirms and many a managerial quick fix are concerned with staffs. How to structure? How to strategize? How to coordinate, integrate, motivate? These all are questions that arise from the sheer presence in megafirms of great numbers of people who provide support, service, and advice but contribute nothing directly to the product of the enterprise.

Small businesses have neither staff nor the kind of support services that staff provide. In a small business, there is no one to liaise, facilitate, coordinate, analyze, advise, or strategize; there is only room (and resources) for workers. Even those who manage must do their share of the work. To the observer accustomed to the bureaucracy of a megafirm, with its cadre of corporate types, small businesses seem to lack the necessary "administrative procedures and controls." They are said to be weak in "downstream product support" and unable to provide "long-term service subsistence." Supporters of small businesses argue that the supposedly sophisticated product and process systems of the megafirms merely add costs and frustrate service/delivery more often than they facilitate it. There is a case to be made on both sides. What is agreed is that the products and processes of the megafirms differ from small businesses in large part because the latter simply don't have all of the people the megafirms have. What is not so often noted is that the people in small businesses are in the business in very different ways and, more often than not, they are different people.

The average small business is a family business. As a funeral home operator observed, "The business and the family are no different; they're one and the same. My dad or brother or I are always here at all times, twenty-four hours a day, 365 days a year. That's how this business has to be run." Even when a small business grows beyond the mom-and-pop, father-and-son/daughter stage, family employees may still predominate as grandchildren, in-laws, and distant relations are drawn into the fold. Of the seventy-five employees at Henry Braza's H&L Tool Company in Madison Heights, Michigan, seven are related to Henry—a wife, daughter, son-in-law, brother, and three grandchildren. Two score more have relatives working there. Staffs of the two Kabob & Kurry Indian restaurants in north Texas are entirely family and extended family members—all thirty-one of them. These are not isolated examples; most small businesses have similar employee profiles, drawing heavily on family, extended family, and friends.

Many of these family businesses are headed by women and minorities, unlikely faces in the boardrooms and executive suites of most megafirms. But small businesses, especially in the service sector, present very few entry barriers to women and minorities, and those barriers that do exist are easily overcome by an investment of sweat equity. Today, women own nearly one-fourth of the sole proprietorships in America and the number is growing. In one-fifth of the states, the number of black businesses has increased more than 60 percent over the last five years. Mexican-Americans and Asian-Americans are beginning to show similar gains in business ownership, especially in the West and Southwest. Another distinguishing characteristic of small-business America is youth at the top. Small-business owner/operators are younger than their *Fortune* 500 counterparts by ten to fifteen years. The real work force of America is best described as not exclusively old, not exclusively white, not exclusively male, and most of all, not exclusively in the employ of corporate giants.

These demographics mean that the typical small business has a work force that looks dramatically different from that found in the megafirms. It behaves differently, too. The corporate giants are established social institutions. Almost tribal in their orientation, IBM, AT&T, GM, and the other 497 of *Fortune's* 500 are replete with their own legends and lore, heroes and habits, traditions and taboos. Employees aren't so much hired as they are initiated. College graduates and MBAs are recruited into these companies, entering as a "class" of trainees. The trainees are then indoctrinated through a vigorous socialization program intended to inculcate them with the mores of the megafirm and prepare them for paths up the career ladder. In the megafirms, an individual's career path is as likely to be determined by corporate politics as by his or her performance. Megafirms are political organizations, and political concerns dictate business behavior. The pragmatic question is how to play the politics. Advice is plentiful as best-sellers tell would-be megafirm careerists everything they didn't learn at the Harvard Business School that they need to know to climb the corporate ladder—from how to dress to what to order for lunch.

But how real are the politics of big business for the rest of us? Larry Stanley, the owner of Empire Bolt and Screw Company, observes, "In big business, they're so concerned with the internal political process—with proving they're worthy of that next promotion—that they don't ever see much of the real world."

Graeme Miller, who left a megafirm to start a small venture capital firm, says, "I couldn't go back to the corporate politics. Now I realize that in a large company, half your time is spent in work and the other half playing politics. What I have now is different, it's fun, more of what business is supposed to be about."

The real world of people in small businesses is much more like a family. Much of that stems from the fact, noted earlier, that often the employees of small businesses are members of the family. Even when a small business must go outside the family for help, it does not/cannot play the numbers game of hiring the way the megafirms do. Large corporations hire newly minted MBAs into classes of thirty or so trainees. They can count on ten leaving after two years and ten more after five years. Of the remaining ten, eight will plateau at middle management and two will have productive careers as top executives in the corporation. In a small business, hiring is much more personal, usually one-on-one. There are no college recruiters, no trainee classes, no training programs, no predetermined career paths. A small business takes on a new employee not because it has historically hired thirty new people every August or because it anticipates management turnover five years hence. A small business hires because it needs someone *now*. Typically, recruiting is by word of mouth, the friend of a friend, the daughter of a customer, the salesman let go by a supplier. Once on board, these new hires are put immediately to work and held accountable for results. Small businesses cannot afford the slack needed for "trainee positions," rotational assignments, or staff specialists. Employees have to be contributing quickly and in a variety of ways. The work force is much more flexible than in a megafirm, where sheer size and functional specialization tend to isolate people early on. Small-business employees typically know the total operation; in the megafirms, workers know only their own narrow territories.

Because employees in small businesses are not isolated from one another, relationships are very different from those in megafirms. As Thomas P. Murphy of *Forbes* observes: "Encounters are frequent and relationships are frequently intense. There is no place to hide from people you don't like or who don't happen to like you. The luxuries of transfers to distant offices, promotions upstairs, and all of the expensive, feather-smoothing stratagems that keep the peace in the big-business world are not available to small companies. You get along with the family. Or you get out."

In a small business, people get along or they get out. In the megafirms, people *get by* whether or not they get along. As in the case of time and money, products and processes, so it is with people. The essential difference between the megafirms that mythically dominate business and the real world of small business is a question of sustenance versus survival. Megafirms sustain themselves—their estimable resources, their product-and-process support systems, their people, and their politics are all directed toward the long-term sustenance of the institution. For the small business, profit, products, and people are all issues of survival, harshly felt by everyone involved. It is this *involvement* in a small business that sets its people apart from those of the megafirm.

Current popular attention to business and management has been hailed by most observers as much needed and long overdue. Attention to business and management is needed—it is an individual and social agenda of unquestioned importance—but it must be attention to business as it actually is, not as it is imagined to be. Exaggerating the scale of business, as currently popular treatments of the subject do, only exacerbates the problems of managers. The myth of the megafirm promotes a perception of business in which every company is a *Fortune* 500 concern with unlimited financial resources, every manager is an omniscient and omnipotent CEO and every employee an aspiring careerist aggressively climbing the corporate ladder. So long as the myth of the megafirm persists, businesses will continue to look to America's corporate giants for methods to improve business management. The business press will continue to devote 95 percent of its linage to less than 2 percent of American businesses. The business schools will continue to turn out 70,000 MBAs annually, trained to be megafirm minions. And the quick fixers will continue to promote megafirm management practices as panaceas for all that ails American businesses of any kind and every size. All of this will reinforce the myth and all of this will miss the mark.

Very little of what is promoted about big business today has any relevance for the business world most of us know as owners, managers, employees, and customers. Most Americans live and work in a small-business world. Most know on a first-name basis the people they work for and with, and chances are, they are related to some, most, or all. Most have a hands-on awareness of how the business is doing, and an intimate knowledge of the relationship between the fortunes of the enterprise and their own. And, what's more, most people like it that way.

It is simply naïve, chauvinistic, and more than a bit imperialistic to suggest that the management practices of successful megafirms apply with equal effectiveness (or apply at all) to every managerial experience. Welsh and White concluded "A Small Business Is Not a Little Big Business" with this observation: "Owner-management of a small business is a distinct discipline characterized by severe constraints on financial resources, a lack of trained personnel, and a short-range management perspective imposed by a volatile competitive environment. Liquidity must be a prime objective. *The analytical models of big business are of limited use in this arena.*" (Italics mine.)

As a general rule, unless business practices emerge from and are consistent with the arena of application, they are likely to be of questionable value. The quick fixes that emerge from megafirms assume resources, support systems, and people that simply don't exist in small businesses. It is analogous to the effort to transport Japanese management methods to the West—the least of the problems is the language barrier! There is a similar gap between megafirms and small businesses, a gap that most managers and workers find frustrating. The myth of the megafirm promotes the promise of managerial magic, but it is a promise that cannot be fulfilled, a promise the pursuit of which is ultimately futile. Few are going to rush to the aid of the managers of small businesses; the quick fixers have their sights set much higher.

As with virtually everything else about his business, the small-business manager is going to have to fix his managerial ills himself, without the myth of the megafirm and its management practices, which are likely to be a misfit. This caution is difficult to heed. Nowhere is the urgency to manage *better, sooner* more acutely felt than among the owners and managers of small businesses. In these times of rapid technological change, rising costs, foreign competition, a changing work force, managers of even the most stable and successful economic institutions long for simple, guaranteed solutions. It is all too tempting to look to what has worked for others and assume that it will work for you.

Economist Lester Thurow captured the keenly felt sense that something is wrong with American management when he wrote:

> America is not experiencing a benevolent second industrial revolution but a long-run economic decline that will affect its ability to competitively produce goods and services for world markets. If American industry fails, the managers are ultimately accountable. While we cannot fire all of America's managers any more than we can fire the American work force, there is clearly something wrong with management. That "something" is going to have to be corrected if America is to compete in world markets.[6]

The urgency to do something—anything—to improve management accounts for the unprecedented attention to the practices of the successful corporate giants in spite of serious questions about the appropriateness of these practices for business as most of us know it. Advice to move with more deliberation gives way to demands for managerial magic *now*. It may be easier to move cautiously if we realize that at the same time that consultants are promoting the magic of megafirms, they are touting the advantages of "getting small." It is the "myth of entrepreneurial management."

4

The Myth of
Entrepreneurial Management

Entrepreneur—a distinctive, confident, and long-
lasting fragrance, creatively blended of exotic
musk, amber, herbs, and Oriental spices with the
subtle accent of cognac.

—*Ad copy for Entrepreneur cologne, 1985*

There was a time in the history of American business when entrepreneurs were the personification of economic evil. The most
successful of these independent businessmen—men like Carnegie,
Rockefeller, Harriman, Mellon, Kennedy—were thought of as
robber barons, profiteers who pillaged America for their own
greed and glory. Those who were less successful were seen as
little more than back-door businessmen, sleazy promoters of
sucker scams, hucksters of hot air—like Professor Harold Hill,
the infamous "Music Man."

From our current perspective, the era of entrepreneurs as evil-
doers seems like a time long, long ago. But it was not so long
ago, no more than thirty years, when to call a businessman an
entrepreneur was a near insult. The fifties were about fitting in,
conforming to the cut of the Corporate Cloth (which was gray
flannel). To be a maverick, to run counter to the crowd was bad,
to be small was bad, to take risks was bad. Entrepreneurs seemed
to embody *all* that was bad—small, risk-taking, independent
businessmen.

Now, thirty years later, entrepreneurship has a whole new

meaning. According to *INC.* magazine, the magazine for entrepreneurs: "Entrepreneurship now means anything that is better than it was before, a synonym for achievement, quality, and taste. It is a source of power and money, a touchstone for creativity, a way to excitement and fame. Business schools now teach it, sociologists study it, and politicians left and right lay claim to having fostered it." Today you can study entrepreneurship at over 250 colleges and universities (up from only sixteen in 1970), or watch the entrepreneur's cable channel. You can buy Entrepreneur cologne or follow the exploits of entrepreneurs on daily soap operas. You can even take your family to Enterprise Square USA, an Oklahoma City amusement park, where you can meet famous entrepreneurial characters from history like Henry Ford, Helena Rubenstein, Sebastian Kresge, or George Washington Carver.

The spirit of entrepreneurship that has captured the American public has not been lost on corporate America. Many of America's largest corporations have gone to great lengths to present their products as the embodiment of the small, independent, underdog efforts we associate with entrepreneurs. In the Bartles and Jaymes commercials for wine coolers, entrepreneurs Frank Bartles and Ed Jaymes speak with down-home naïveté and sincerity of their efforts to make a premium product from modest means. It is an appealing message, one that taps into the American fascination with the little guy making good—the independent, underdog entrepreneur. Never mind that Frank and Ed were "created" by the giant ad agency Ogilvy and Mather to be spokespersons for Bartles and Jaymes, the wine coolers produced by Ernest and Julio Gallo, the country's largest distiller. Whither entrepreneurship?

So powerful is the entrepreneur image today that even the largest, most institutional of enterprises attempt to capture some of the entrepreneurial mystique. Rockwell International has run a television and magazine campaign featuring the copy "Rockwell International managers have the entrepreneurial freedom to move through the maze." Rockwell president Donald Beall explains the company's desire to be seen as vital, innovative, creative. "When you think of entrepreneur, maybe you think of a couple of guys in a garage coming up with the latest Silicon Valley wonder product. Or someone like Mrs. Fields, who turned the freshly baked cookie into a mini-industry. I'd like you to think of an entrepreneur not as a lone wolf starting a small business, but as someone who works for Rockwell."

Rockwell is not alone in its efforts to be seen as an entrepreneurial enterprise. Commercials, product presentations, and recruitment advertisements are used by many of America's largest, most successful, and most stable companies to convince potential customers and employees that they embody the spirit of entrepreneurship and all that entails. Goodyear, Raytheon, Hewlett-Packard, Corning, Pitney-Bowes, Centel Corporation, even the state of Arizona, all want to be seen as places where individuals are able to pursue ideas in the spirit of entrepreneurship.

Our fascination with entrepreneurs goes much deeper than this marketing mystique. The belief that entrepreneurs are more creative, more innovative, more committed, more cost-conscious has led to a number of entrepreneurial-oriented "quick fixes"— management methods for bringing to any organization the benefits and virtues ascribed to small businesses. Rosabeth Kanter, the noted organizational observer, author, and consultant, has characterized this uncritical embracing of entrepreneurial management as "a managerial liberation movement that will automatically result in leaner, self-directed organizations with lower overhead and a proliferation of profitable new products and techniques." The four central tenets in the entrepreneurial management movement are (1) downsize, (2) decentralize, (3) participate, and (4) innovate. The myth of entrepreneurship has led many managers to embrace these tenets with little regard for the realities of their application. A closer look at these core entrepreneurial elements reveals that contrary to the modern management myth, it may be neither easy nor effective for organizations and managers to be entrepreneurial.

Michael J. Kami, popular strategic consultant, looking at the overall economic outlook for the last quarter of the decade, issued the following advice for his subscriber companies: "Develop great cost-consciousness in your organization: Lean, leaner, leanest." Kami's advice captures the conventional wisdom of the time. The admonition to get smaller and get stronger emerged from the 1981–82 recession and has been an anchor axiom of managerial advisers throughout the decade. The lean-and-mean metaphor likened American companies to champion boxers who had become fat and complacent and needed to trim down to fighting weight.

Trimming down means eliminating people and positions any way you cut it, although Corporatespeak has offered a number of creative euphemisms for the process—skinnying down, demassing, delayering, demanning, downsizing, and restructuring, to mention only a few. By any name, the practice, once viewed as traumatic, is now very much in vogue. Companies that have embraced the latest corporate fitness craze include General Electric, DuPont, Eastman Kodak, H. J. Heinz, Lever Brothers, U.S. Steel, Polaroid, Apple Computers, AT&T, Ford, Union Carbide, CBS—the list goes on and on. Eugene E. Jennings, a Michigan State University professor who has studied corporate staffing, found that since the beginning of the decade, U.S. companies have eliminated over half a million managers. According to Jennings, "Eighty-nine of our 100 largest corporations—perhaps more—have gone to total corporate realignments."

The reasons for downsizing are many. Rising costs and diminishing margins have made the elimination of managerial fat a *necessary* move for some companies. Technology improvements, especially in the area of data processing, have made the elimination of managerial layers *possible* for many other companies. Pronouncements by management consultants of the productivity and marketing ("close to the customers") gains to be garnered from downsizing have made the process *desirable* to many CEOs. Paint all of this against a background of unprecedented popularity of entrepreneurs, and almost any and every company can find ample reason for reductions. Certainly there is no lack of those who are direct in advising companies to get small. Thirty years ago, Peter Drucker argued that there was no excuse for a business to have more than six levels of management. Today, Tom Peters has taken up the drumbeat: "Productivity, spirit, and general corporate effectiveness go up as the size of the headquarters staff goes down." Such proclamations are clearly popular in board-rooms, but the relationship between size and productivity may not be quite so clear-cut.

To be sure, there are dramatic downsizing success stories, companies that serve as an example to all for their excellence and, it is argued, not coincidentally, their elimination of excess. Dow Chemical Company operates without organization charts because Paul F. Oreffice, president and CEO, believes that charts stifle interaction and creativity. MCI Communications Corporation has charts, but William McGowan, MCI chairman, doesn't fill all of the positions. "We believe that the fewer levels of management we have, and the more direct our lines of communication are, the more productive we are." Schlumberger, the giant in the "wireline" business used by oil companies to record and analyze prospects, has no single central headquarters, no strategic planning department, no marketers, and no teams of corporate lawyers. Of Schlumberger's nearly 75,000 employees worldwide, only about 200, or one-third of 1 percent, work in central administration. Mars Inc., the $4-billion candy company, has been lauded for running its sixty divisions with a corporate staff of just twenty people.

These and other comparable success stories certainly suggest that smaller is better, and beyond these anecdotes there is some supportive research. The Chicago-based consulting firm A. T. Kearny Inc. studied twenty-six top performing companies and fifteen lesser performers. They found that the twenty-six stars averaged 7.2 management levels while the lesser lights averaged 11.1.[1] The implication is that reducing management levels leads to increased sales and earnings growth. No wonder management cuts have become so popular!

Just as fad diets often shortchange devotees nutritionally, sometimes to the detriment of their health, faddish management efforts to get lean and mean can cut perilously close to the bone *without* automatic increases in productivity. Ira T. Kay, a partner with the Hay Group Inc., reports that consulting firm's study of the pharmaceutical industry. "The company with the highest profits, while leaner than most of its peers, was far from the leanest organization in our sample. Our other industry studies show that 'fatness' or 'leanness' often varies across staff function. The same organization that is overstaffed by 30 percent in finance may be understaffed by 20 percent in personnel. Maximal profitability results from *optimal*, not minimal staffing."[2]

The difference between optimal and minimal staffing is often lost in the enthusiasm to be entrepreneurlike. The real key to organizational form for any company is not de facto delayering, demassing, or downsizing; it is, instead, having the simplest structure (fewest management layers) that will allow the necessary operating decisions to be made efficiently and effectively. Management professor and consultant Charles W. Hofer suggests that appropriate staff size is a function of "(A) keeping the staff small enough and productive enough so that line management always controls both strategies and tactics, and (B) keeping the staff large enough to give accurate and timely advice on all key actions and decisions."[3]

Even among the championed lean and mean, there is evidence to suggest that where staffing is concerned, minimal may not be optimal. Consider Schlumberger, hailed for its profits and parsimonious staffing. A key Schlumberger staffer, Claude Baks, was hired by Mark Schlumberger as an engineer in 1946 but never had any official duties to the time of his retirement at age sixty-five. Yet he could enter any meeting, anywhere at Schlumberger, and he reported only to chairman Jean Riboud. Riboud described the critical staff role played by Baks: "He has never had a title in thirty-five years. He has never had a secretary. He has never written a letter. . . . He forces people to think. His main contribution to Schlumberger has been to prevent Schlumberger from becoming an establishment."[4] Ill-defined staff jobs, such as Baks's, are expendable in lean organizations.

Scores of companies, large and small, have eliminated apparently redundant managers, expendable staff, unnecessary para-professionals only to find after the fact either that too many people have been cut or that the wrong people have been cut. Few organization observers are so naïve as to presume that organization charts depict accurately how information flows and how tasks are coordinated, yet in the rush to get lean and mean, the corporate cutters seldom look beyond the organization chart to see what people are *really* doing. Rosabeth Kanter recounts the story of a small airline that assumed the manager of schedules and routes was just a watchdog over clerks who could do the task themselves. "Several months later—when travel costs to move people around the system had mounted, overtime had gone sky-high, and the union was upset—the company discovered that it was the 'redundant' manager who had held the whole thing together."[5]

Large staffs are said by some to be a residue of accelerated World War II production schedules when efficiency was irrelevant. Others point to the spawning of huge numbers of MBAs in the 1970s as the source of overblown staffs—when the complexity of problems increased, the response of many organizations was to increase staff to fix it. Staffs conduct studies that beget more staff. Some companies have historically resisted the trends by making an effort at the outset to start lean and stay lean. People Express adopted as part of its charter the vision of founder and chairman Don Burr "to try and develop a better way for people to work together. We thought longer and harder about building our people structure here than we did anything else."

The result of Burr's vision at People Express was a structure and staffing unique in the airline industry, indeed, unique in corporate America. Richard Hackman, Yale professor and consultant to People Express, observed: "Other firms have done parts of what they're doing, but the complete package is unique. They're trying to invent a new way of organizing and managing the human resources of the firm." The new way was to be lean and mean from the beginning and stay that way. At People Express initially, there were only three levels of management. In order to eliminate supervisory intervention, managers were organized into work teams of two or three managers. There were no staff positions, no specialists. People Express recruited and hired only three categories of personnel—flight managers (pilots), maintenance managers, and customer service managers. Cross-utilization and job rotation were key elements in the People strategy—every manager (all employees had the manager title) was required to spend some portion of time outside his/her primary area of responsibility each month. Even their ads trumpeted their trim approach: "The next time you fly People Express, your coffee may be served by People's chief financial officer, Bob McAdoo, who is a certified flight attendant and flies weekly."

Minimal bureaucracy, group organization of workers, rotation of staff through a variety of jobs—there was no fat at People Express. Industry executives and consultants were fascinated with the lean, flexible structure that seemed to be key to People's initial success. And in the early days, minimal did appear to be optimal. But over time there were costs. The flat structure worked well with 200 employees because problems could be dealt with personally; at 2,000 employees, the lean structure was overburdened and unwieldy. Eschewing staff specialists, People did not develop sophisticated computer, telephone-reservation, or baggage-handling systems. This aggravated problems of loose management control. Job rotation made employees jacks-of-all-trades and masters of none; they gave up depth of knowledge and often commitment to quality performance as well. At People Express the optimal soon became obsolete. William Fonvielle, vice-president of Goodmeasure Inc., a Cambridge, Massachusetts, consulting firm, sums up the lesson on lean to be learned from People Express: "The real issue is whether any given style or approach is appropriate for any organization throughout its lifetime."[6]

It is true that most entrepreneurial organizations are lean in staff, close to their customers. What often goes unsaid is that these small enterprises are *lean by necessity, not by choice*. If they could, many would choose to expand their staffs so that they could benefit from the information and analyses such staffs can generate. This is not to suggest that they would automatically be more productive and more profitable were they not so lean: much depends upon how the added information and analyses are put to use. By the same measure, it should not be assumed that staffing in the lean style of entrepreneurs will make the megafirms or organizations of any size more profitable. The issue, again, is *optimal* structure: staff will differ from situation to situation. Popular dictates toward lean, leaner, leanest don't automatically mean good, better, best. Available research and the experience of companies like People Express provide some more sophisticated guides for finding the optimal structure and staff for an organization. For example, strategy and size go hand in hand. As a firm's strategy becomes more complex, so must its structure if it is not to suffer major declines in economic performance. The obituary at People Express from an industry observer reads, "If People wanted to remain a small counterculture airline, they could have gotten away with it longer."[7]

The relationship between complexity and size can work within organizations as well. Where operations face conditions such as small, complex, geographically dispersed markets, there may be economy-of-scale potentials that can be fully realized by staff data collection and analysis. This can easily be seen in purchasing departments. In many industries, direct material, parts, and components represent about 80 percent of total manufacturing costs. To maximize volume leverage in its purchasing power, a company needs experienced, skilled staff, and often lots of them, to gather and analyze data to present to vendors. Lean in this critical area can mean loose, and loose can lead to losing. Volatile markets and/or expensive resources present similar opportunities for realizing economies of scale that can only be captured with a buildup in staff.

Beyond strategy and situation, timing can make a difference in the optimal size of a company. Where clearly evident medium- to long-term needs are present, a gradual buildup of staff is in order. If staff-skilled employees are at the same time trained and knowledgeable in operational areas, their skills can be transferred to operational jobs as the needs for staff diminish. In most other special- and short-term-need instances, outside consultants may be more appropriate than the buildup of internal staffs.

In the rush to emulate entrepreneurs, many companies have cut deep beyond fat into their management muscle. Where structure and size are concerned, minimal is not necessarily optimal. The choice of organization structure and staff size ought to be the result of reason rather than rhetoric. As a final evidential point, consider the case of IBM, judged by many to be *the* single most successful corporation in the world. IBM, too, aspires to staying close to the customer, not by trimming management but by proliferating managers. IBM keeps a small-business atmosphere by limiting the number of employees to each manager. The customary span of control is roughly twelve to one. The result? Forty-five thousand managers! IBM gets the advertised advantages of getting small by getting very large.

In 1985, Tom Peters wrote, "American industry is well into what I like to call 'radical decentralization,' a process in which the lines and boxes on organization charts are being reconfigured in order to permanently confer authority on line organizations."[8] Radical decentralization, the dispersal of the power to make decisions to the lowest-level managers, follows naturally from the elimination of staff and management layers. Fewer decision makers means the remaining decisions must be further dispersed. Such a move is also consistent with the desire to emulate entrepreneurs by keeping decision making as close to the action—the producing and selling action—as possible. Radical decentralization is in vogue today, but radical decentralization may not automatically result in improved efficiency and effectiveness (radical decentralization *may not even be entrepreneurial*).

For as long as there have been organizations, there has been the question, "What should be decided where, by whom?" It is a question of centralization—power for decision making in the hands of a single, high-level executive—versus decentralization—power to make decisions transferred to lower-level managers. Actually, these are not two separate concepts but, instead, opposite ends of a continuum. Historically, sentiment in American business has swung from one end to the other, almost decade by decade. In the fifties, centralization was in vogue; in the sixties, decentralization returned to popularity. Centralization came back to dominance in the seventies but gave way to decentralization in the eighties. Each of these swings should be appreciated in its historical context. Centralization in the fifties was an extension of integrative and coordinating mechanisms introduced during the war years. In the sixties, decentralization mirrored the democratization of the workplace and demands for participation. The centralization trend in the seventies was consistent with conglomerates' aggressive acquisition strategies and their consequent needs for coordination. And today, the fascination with the entrepreneur and all that is entrepreneurial has thrust decentralization back into prominence. Except now, in keeping with the need to package management practices, it is the "new, improved, radical decentralization."

What does a radically decentralized company look like? Curtice-Burns Inc., the food manufacturer, is an example. Its headquarters staff of only twelve people, located in Rochester, New York, oversees seven divisions through a decentralized organization structure. Each division is considered a profit center, and each division's chief executive is completely responsible for the division. Completely delegated authority is the rule except in the area of major capital investments. Each division chief must transmit requests for funds for capital improvements to the company's board of directors. Apart from this one constraint, each division is an autonomous unit with the authority to make all the decisions necessary to running an independent business. Hugh Cumming, president and CEO, believes decentralization has been a major contributor to Curtice-Burns's success.[9]

In companies like Curtice-Burns, much is made of the autonomy afforded individual operating managers. It is said that autonomy makes managers behave like entrepreneurs. Aspiring to this entrepreneurial spirit, many companies, large and small, have made the move toward decentralization. When General Foods was emphasizing cost control, a central management committee made virtually all of the decisions regarding new products, advertising, and capital spending. Today the emphasis at General Foods is on product innovation and diversification, and those decisions have been delegated to middle management. Strategic business units in coffee and prepackaged foods have been granted full divisional status with direct control over sales, purchasing, testing new products, advertising, and capital expenditures. The aim is for a more aggressive, entrepreneurial culture at General Foods.

Decentralization at Sears has been driven by an attempt to reduce the highest overhead costs in retailing—nearly 30 percent of each sales dollar goes to overhead and administrative expenses. Sears hopes that driving decision making downward in the organization will drive costs down.

At Flambeau Corporation, founder Bill Sauey was forced to decentralize in order to continue his aggressive acquisition strategy: "I was killing myself trying to manage 500 employees spread out in five plants around the country running three shifts a day." When Sauey acquired Vlchek Plastics Company, he let it operate under the authority of its own general manager instead of merging it into the central organization as he had always done with previous acquisitions. "But I didn't this time because I was so busy with the rest of the company—that I knew if I brought it into our system, I'd screw it up."[10]

Rewards of efficiency, cost control, and entrepreneurial behavior are routinely promised to those who decentralize. The risks are rarely made explicit but they are estimable. If there is a risk that an owner-founder-manager like Bill Sauey can "screw it up," imagine the risk run in a fully decentralized organization—risks that some who have rushed to decentralize radically have come to know only too well. Many companies that have gone to the extreme in transferring decision-making power from corporate to the divisions and operating units have experienced some dysfunctional, even debilitating, side effects. Interdivisional rivalries are often exacerbated by decentralization, as incentives to coordinate efforts and cooperate across divisional or even unit boundaries are often lost. Lost, too, is the big picture. Under radical decentralization, no one feels responsibility for the long-term or across-the-corporation concerns. The development of technology, R&D, the development of people, training, the development of long-range positioning, and planning suffer because everyone is willing to "let Harry do it." Radical decentralization can also put the company at risk in critical exposure areas such as resource acquisition, labor relations, or regulatory adherence. An unknowing, uncaring, or unthinking operating manager can jeopardize an entire corporation at a cost that far outweighs any benefit that might accrue from entrepreneurlike decision making at the lowest possible level.

Somewhere between the promised rewards of decentralization and the potential risks lies reality. It is an in-between proposition. For the majority of managers, there is neither absolute centralization nor absolute decentralization. An organization may be relatively centralized in some functions or operations and, at the same time, relatively decentralized in others. Westinghouse is a case in point. All strategic decisions for the $10-billion company are made centrally—what businesses to be in, what to strive for in those businesses. Base pricing and share of the market standing are the two centrally decided measures applied to all thirty Westinghouse divisions. Tactical decisions are made by managers closest to the product or point of sale. When television station WJZ in Baltimore decided to cooperate with local police in an anticrime project, the station manager committed the station on his own authority. Similarly, when Daniel Soraka developed Westinghouse's first robot, funds for that project were made available through his managers. However, where Westinghouse must ensure standard policies and procedures, such as in the areas of quality, personnel, and finance, operations are centralized. For example, in 1982, Westinghouse began a company-wide program to use specialized techniques, such as quality circles, to improve product quality. In 1983, the company reached a three-year agreement with the labor unions that represent its 48,000 employees. The quality program and the labor contracts are centralized because of their long-term importance to the company.

Westinghouse shows a reasoned response to the question of centralization versus decentralization that is in sharp contrast to the knee-jerk response of those swayed by the rhetoric of radical decentralization. There *are* reasonable ways to resolve the question of where any organization should be on the centralization/decentralization continuum. The first step in deciding on the appropriate degree of decentralization is to frame the question properly. As centralization/decentralization is not an all-or-nothing issue, the proper perspective is one that asks *what* operations or functions should be centralized or decentralized and *to what degree.*

In the decision of what to decentralize and to what degree, managers ought to be guided by some key considerations. The acknowledged advantages of centralization are control, coordination, and a comprehensive context. Where the organization faces critical uncertainties—i.e., performance criteria, resource availability and utilization, key regulatory or contractual exposures—the need for *control* is high and a greater degree of centralization is in order. Even the most avid corporate proponents of decentralization, companies such as GM, DuPont, GE, Sears, and Marriott, maintain centralized collection and analysis of performance data, areas affording corporate control.

Within and across functions and operations, organizations may be presented with significant economy-of-scale and *coordination* opportunities. Typical examples of such opportunities can be found in purchasing, training, and research and development areas. The importance of these areas to the total corporation is too great to be given over to the divisions. At the same time, the costs of these activities are too great to be borne by individual functions or operating units. Complete decentralization results in duplication of effort and destroys the synergy of coordination.

Every company faces critical uncertainties about the future. These uncertainties require long-range planning in the context of the corporate whole. Territorial concerns constrain division thinking about possibilities on the up- and downside. Divisions can become myopic about immediate operating issues—so much so that the next quarter is as far away as they can think. The greater the need for a *comprehensive* look at the business at any point in time, present or future, the greater the need for centralization.

As a company, large or small, assesses its need for control, coordination, and a comprehensive context, one important moderating variable has to be kept in mind—*confidence in subordinate managers.* The degree to which a CEO has confidence in his subordinates' understanding of the corporate philosophy and practices, and in their ability to implement them, will determine how comfortable he is with pushing decision making down in the organization at the possible risk to control, coordination, and a comprehensive context. In the absence of such confidence, decentralization is not an option, no matter how important it might be to generate entrepreneurial behavior.

The degree of centralization or decentralization is properly a product of corporate calculation and choice—not a campaign war cry. The choice is conditioned by the context in which the organization operates and by the capabilities of its people, the same elements that condition effective implementation of the other management practices associated with entrepreneurial management.

One of the most impressive things about doing business with an effective small business—be it a dry cleaner, a donut shop, or a data analysis concern—is the personal involvement of the employees. They all know the business; they know what is important to the business; and they seem genuinely to care about the customer. Experiences with small, entrepreneurial businesses often confirm what has long been known about the relationship between participation and commitment: when people have a sense of involvement in something, they are more committed to it and will work longer, harder, and smarter for it.

In yet another attempt to capture some of the entrepreneurial atmosphere in megafirms, management consultants today have touted a variety of participative devices from worker advisory councils to worker-management participative teams to, at the extreme, employee ownership. All of these participative efforts are aimed at increased worker involvement and enhanced quality and quantity of productivity, which are presumed to follow. Without doubt the most popular of participative programs have been quality circles (QCs). The members of a quality circle meet regularly to solve common problems. The circles usually meet for an hour once a week on company time. The circle objectives are typically quality improvement, productivity enhancement, and employee participation; they do not focus on personal gripes and problems.

A list of companies employing QCs or a variant thereof reads like a *Who's Who* in American business: IBM, General Motors, Westinghouse, Union Carbide, Lockheed, Northrup Aircraft, American Express, Motorola, TRIO, Hewlett-Packard, Texas Instruments, Eastman Kodak, Procter & Gamble, Digital Equipment, Honeywell, Xerox, and the list goes on.

By 1986 the International Association of Quality Circles had over 6,000 QCs registered, but there are at least that many more employee-participation programs not exclusively identified with quality. For example, Control Data has involvement teams; Tektronics uses Tekcircles; Union Carbide has employee PRIDE circles for Productivity through Recognition, Involvement and Development of Employees.

By any name, the reputed benefits of structured employee participation programs are many: increased communication between management and employees; increased commitment to the organization; enhanced development of employees; improved employee satisfaction; more innovation. Anecdotal evidence suggests that, at least in some areas, the promised rewards of participative programs pay out. Before the Participative Management Program (PMP) was introduced at Motorola's electroplating operation in 1980, only six ounces of gold for every ten ounces purchased made it into the final product. The company turned the problem over to a group of experts—the division's own employees. Within four months, a PMP team had identified fifty-one places in the production process where gold was being lost. They saved the company $3 million the first year.

The Campbell Soup Company has instituted more than 500 quality circles of production-line employees at various plants and asked them to focus on getting production costs down. One circle, at a frozen food processing plant in Modesto, California, figured out how to reduce down time on a particularly expensive piece of equipment, thereby saving Campbell $300,000 a year. Another employee group, at an ingredient plant in Milwaukee, streamlined its manufacturing process, saving the company about $250,000 a year.

Employees on the F-5 assembly line at Northrup Aircraft had long complained of dull drill bits. The usual response was "Get a new bit." When one of the circles studied this problem, they found that some bits would break before drilling one hole, while other bits efficiently drilled hundreds of holes before they needed to be reworked. Circle members recommended tightening rework tolerances on used bits and management agreed. The result was several thousand dollars saved in that one department.

At Boise Cascade, employee groups were challenged to come up with ideas to cut salary and overhead expenses by 3 percent. In every area, the groups did better than that. There were some layoffs but more often employees figured out ways to cut costs without cutting jobs.

These examples typify reports from participative management efforts in that they highlight cost reductions as a result of increased worker involvement. Less often chronicled are the costs *of* getting workers involved.

Mechanisms for making management more participative date back to experiments in the early days of management science. Before QCs, the most widely touted participation scheme was the Scanlon Plan—a cost-savings share plan utilizing worker committees—conceived in 1937. The popularity of participative management in the eighties has been in response to the need to compete against foreign imports. But researcher William Cooke, professor at the University of Michigan, reports, "About 75 percent of all programs in the early 1980s failed." Why? Largely for the same reason they failed in the earlier era: lack of management support. For participative management to work, management must relinquish power to the workers. In organizations, information is power, and managers, in controlling access to information, control power. In order to participate effectively, workers must be given access to information—production numbers, costs, margins, and so on. The idea of sharing this information, and thereby sharing power, hasn't sat well with most managers.

The case of Boeing Aerospace's manufacturing division, with 300 managers spread through four organizational levels, has been fairly typical. The division's initial thrust at participation in 1980 was to put together troubleshooting teams of workers, engineers, and managers to smooth bumps in production. Other middle managers often perceived the teams as intruders, and the idea flopped. "The only thing that remained was a negative attitude about employee involvement," notes Carl Hicks, head of quality improvement in the division. "We're still trying to undo that damage." In 1984, Boeing tried again, this time with more involvement from middle managers and, consequently, with greater success. The lesson from Boeing is that it often takes years for participative structures to generate participative behaviors.

General Electric's experience over twenty years demonstrates how difficult it is to get management to support participative programs consistently. GE began experimenting in the late 1960s and by 1975 had work teams in twelve plants. The experiment survived in only one plant. Everywhere else the programs fell victim to layoffs, management rotation, and executive oversight. "This is *hard* stuff, changing all those headsets," notes Gary Kissler, a human resources manager in the company's lighting group. He blames GE's slow progress on what he calls "the lack-of-pain issue." Managers who think that their businesses are producing acceptable results aren't particularly interested in changing their ways.[11]

Changing management "headsets" is not the only obstacle to

making the workplace more participative; management skills must be altered as well. Philip Ricco, productivity director at S. C. Johnson and Son Inc., of Racine, Wisconsin, says that the problem of getting managers to make the transition from traditional authoritarian/autocratic management of individuals to the facilitation of worker teams "is huge. It's *the* problem." James Lester, president of Eggers Industries Inc., a midwestern building products company, says, "The participative manager needs better management skills and people skills. Most of those things aren't trainable."

Lester's perspective has led to the reassignment of supervisors and managers who could not change their style into positions that don't involve worker participation. However, most companies do not have the latitude to make reassignments on a grand scale, and so they have invested heavily in retraining, recognizing that without new management skills, participative programs will never get beyond the point of proclamation. Extensive training programs have been instituted to get managers skilled at and comfortable with facilitating worker groups. In the most comprehensive programs, training has been reinforced with other measures. Some companies, like Florida Power and Light, provide special tutors for those managers who have difficulty making the transition. Others, such as TRW, have tied managers' pay and promotions to their ability at the participative style as an added incentive to change.

Even with top-management dictates, training programs, and incentives, managers and supervisors have resisted moves to more participatory methods. What has emerged in the main has been participative forms without much substance. The requisite committees, circles, advisory groups are duly instituted, usually with a fanfare befitting rollout of a new product. The managers put up with worker participation but rarely provide the support necessary to realize the promise of participation. Workers become cynical when they see that their ability to participate effectively is constrained by when and how management will *allow* them to participate. At worst, participative management is viewed by workers as cooptation.

Harley-Davidson is frequently cited as a quality-circle success story. The only U.S.-based manufacturer of big motorcycles, Harley came back from near bankruptcy in 1981 to a record market share in 1987. Quality circles and other employee-involvement programs have contributed to reduced labor costs—from 3,800 employees in 1980 to 2,000 today—improved quality, and revitalized marketing. Now employee resistance to participative programs is emerging. Union officials feel that quality circles have veered away from their original purpose and have become institutionalized as a way of keeping pressure on the workers. Workers complain that the company is interested only in reductions in production costs that reduce the number of workers.[12]

Other companies have had similar experiences with worker resistance to participation programs. A circle leader from the Lynn, Massachusetts, GE defense plant described the participative program there as the company's attempt to clothe authoritative management in participative dress: "The group felt that management had the plans and was only bringing them to the worker improvement group to get them approved." Such perceptions are heightened where management takes a hard line on what worker groups can and cannot consider. A major participative effort at CIGMA Corporation came to a halt when management, after an extensive effort to solicit employee input, decided the suggested actions were simply too expensive to pursue. When it's okay for workers to recommend cost savings or quality improvement but not grievance procedures or supervisory practices, workers are likely to suspect management's commitment to participation.

In those rare instances (and they are rare) where participatory groups have been implemented with the full commitment of executives, managers, and workers, and with the necessary skills in place, the results may still not be all that has been promised. One reason is that after years of authoritarian management in American businesses, there is a degree of "learned helplessness" among managers and workers alike. Individuals or groups socialized to taking orders don't easily take to independent decision making. GM found its efforts to push decision making down into the organization frustrated by the passivity of the work force. For example, a stamping operation in Pittsburgh had become so reliant on detailed orders from Detroit that plant managers were at a loss when told to set their own goals and solve their own problems.

Another common pattern in participative management and QC efforts is an initial flurry of cost-reducing, quality-improving suggestions, which reflects both the enthusiasm of start-up and the ease of acting on the obvious. As worker groups turn their attention to more fundamental concerns, however, answers come less readily, discussions are more labored, core conflicts surface, enthusiasm wanes, and the process dies a slow, sometimes agonizing death. Such was the experience at Eaton, a high-tech and manufacturing concern that was into participative methods as early as the 1960s. After experiencing measurable improvement in the relationship between labor and management, advances leveled off. By 1986, the chief of industrial relations for Eaton reported: "We plateaued. The plants did not continue the evolution. It didn't go to the next level that I would have pictured: self-managed work groups, or processes that brought decision making down to lower levels."[13]

Reading the popular business press of today, one would conclude that participative methods are truly a panacea born of the times—a way to enhance employee involvement and, thereby, to emulate entrepreneurial commitment in even the largest of organizations. A little knowledge of participative methods proves them to be neither new nor panaceas. Experience has shown that there clearly are advantages to making the workplace more participative, especially in terms of communication and commitment. But experience has also revealed the disadvantages, and these need to be articulated as clearly as the advantages to dispel any myths managers may hold about participation.

Participative methods require skills that differ dramatically from the behaviors managers and workers are accustomed to in their more traditional organizational roles, and this in turn requires active support from top management as well as extensive training. This means participative methods are costly. And even with training and facilitative structures, not everyone will be willing or able to participate. Unwillingness or inability on the part of managers or workers undermines the participative process. Under the best of circumstances, participative methods are time-consuming, conflict-generating, often goal-displacing (deflecting attention from other pursuits), and, potentially, inefficient.

When participation results in recommendations that are consistently rejected and/or ignored, or when participation is merely an opportunity for workers to "rubber stamp" management initiatives (cooptation), the credibility of management is destroyed. Participative methods, at the other extreme, can lead to management abdicating the responsibility to set goals and measure results. In either case participation can degenerate into a complete loss of managerial control.

Small entrepreneurial businesses are participative per force; their size alone dictates that workers are involved, informed, and committed. The popular belief that large organizations can achieve the same qualities through participative methods has some merit to it but some myth as well. As in the case of advice to downsize and to decentralize, managers should look upon the advice to participate with a great deal of caution and with full consideration of the conditions that can make participation an effective management tool or an exercise in futility and frustration.

The record of creativity and innovation established by entrepreneurs and small businesses has been much admired by both those who administer and those who advise corporations. It is yet another area in which the big aspire to be small, asking, "How can we establish the entrepreneurial conditions that foster creativity?" The management Merlins have a ready response—intrapreneuring and skunkworks.

Gifford Pinchot III coined the term *intrapreneur* to describe *intra*corporate entre*preneurs*—employees given the time, money, and freedom from bureaucratic constraints to pursue innovations *within* the corporate framework.[14] Pinchot points to examples such as Hulki Aldikach, the auto designer, who was turned loose by Pontiac to develop his vision of the Fiero—Pontiac's successful new sports car. Another example which has taken on almost legendary proportion in intrapreneuring is that of Art Fry, who invented the now ubiquitous yellow pads with the gently adhesive backs—Post-it Notes—and pushed his creation through 3M.

Peters and Waterman used the same 3M example to describe "skunkworks"—semi-autonomous units within the organization where individuals can have the best of both worlds, corporate and entrepreneurial. Such operations make available to the intrapreneur all the managerial, technological, and financial resources of the big company, but give him or her the independence to run the business largely as an entrepreneur. Typically, intrapreneurs are freed of the standard budgeting and reporting procedures and allowed to start small things that the company can afford to bet on—and can afford to lose on. The corporation provides the venture capital for employees to develop their brainchild. Frequently, the intrapreneur is asked to take some token risks as a measure of his commitment to the project. The requested risk might be for the employee to forgo bonuses or salary increases for the life of the project. The balancing benefit is the corporation's pledge to reward the intrapreneur if the project succeeds and is brought into the mainstream of the corporate product or service line.

Success stories at 3M, Pontiac, Citicorp, Bell Labs, Hewlett-Packard, Johnson & Johnson, IBM, and many other leading corporations have fueled enthusiasm for these entrepreneurial halfway houses. But there are problems as well. In a rush to encourage employees to be entrepreneurial, quantity can displace quality concerns. Limited development funds may be spread thinly over a great number of projects (some trivial) rather than dedicated to high-priority pursuits—invention takes precedence over improvement, products over processes—and fragmentation, dilution, and duplication of effort are often the result.

These problems with intrapreneuring and skunkworks are largely problems of implementation and could be minimized—and in many companies have been minimized—with careful attention to the administration of entrepreneurial programs. There are more fundamental problems with the concept that raise questions as to whether intrapreneuring ought to be addressed so enthusiastically by managers—and even if at all. The first question has to do with just how much innovation and creativity an organization needs. To ask such a question among managers today borders on heresy, yet it needs to be asked. The response is even more heretical. Economist Lester Thurow of Massachusetts Institute of Technology has said: "The current philosophy that if we liberate the entrepreneur, all the problems will disappear, is wrong. . . . If you believe entrepreneurs can solve all the problems by themselves, you'll never do the other things that need to be done to make the system work."[15]

Alfred D. Chandler, Straus Professor of Business History at the Harvard Business School, puts the current popularity of entrepreneurs in historical (and organizational) perspective with this observation: "There have been two earlier entrepreneurial periods. The first was the second industrial revolution of the 1880s and 90s. The second was in the 1920s, when the great entrepreneurs, the Sloans and the Fords, put together their giant enterprises. In those industries, in order to stay in business, you not only had to exploit the technology, you had to build up your organization. Historically, the key entrepreneurial act has been creating an organization."[16]

The important point here is that there are times in the evolution of an organization when innovation and entrepreneurship are desirable and necessary, and other times when they are not. These needs have more to do with the conditions of the marketplace than with what is managerially fashionable. For example, there are industries and markets in which the basics of product and material technology and marketing and distribution methods change very little. Extractive industries like mining and producers of staples such as salt, bread, liquor, and forestry and paper products all use relatively stable resources with proven produc-

tion technologies. In these relatively static economic environments, the most successful companies are those that maximize
operating efficiencies by refining existing strategies and methods.
Major innovation efforts in these companies are not needed and,
indeed, are not desirable inasmuch as they may deflect energies
and resources away from what the company does best.

In those economic environments where there are changes in
resources, product technology, marketing, and distribution, the
successful companies are those that adapt to changes as they occur, by building on their existing strengths. The entire management information computer industry is an example. Here, too,
the value of innovation and creativity is often oversold. In these
dynamic economic environments, change is frequent, but it is
typically incremental, not quantum—modifications are more in
order than are major innovations. Where modifications are not
possible, the organization is confronted with either seeking new
industry opportunities where existing strengths are applicable or
acquiring new strengths. This latter instance describes the *real*
need for innovation in the organization. Clearly these are not the
conditions faced by *all* organizations *all* of the time. The need
for innovation in organizations is a sometime thing and it is not
always best served by encouraging intrapreneurs.

One tangible result of making the entrepreneur the hero of
our times is that he/she has also become the object of scientific
and not-so-scientific scrutiny. As a result, a lot is known about
entrepreneurs and how they operate, and most of what is known
suggests that entrepreneurs won't do well in corporate settings
no matter how autonomous their skunkworks. The Boston-based
research firm McBer and Company, founded by David C.
McClelland, has done extensive work on identifying and validat-
ing the "personal entrepreneurial characteristics" found to predict successful entrepreneurial behavior. From their studies, the
most frequently cited predictors of successful entrepreneurship
include: achievement motivation—a concern with performing
better, more efficiently, against an internal standard of excellence; internal locus of control—belief that success comes from

one's own efforts rather than from forces outside of one's control, such as organizational politics; and attitudes and values—entrepreneurs value independence and autonomy, are open-minded and not authoritarian.

These findings and other psychological portrayals of entrepreneurs suggest that it is the *individual, not the institutional setting,* that spurs entrepreneurial behavior. Anecdotal evidence from entrepreneurial experiences confirms this observation. Abraham Zaleznik, a psychoanalyst who teaches at the Harvard Business School, has said, "To understand the entrepreneur, you first have to understand the psychology of the juvenile delinquent." The analogy is not facetious. The common denominator among entrepreneurs is a drive for autonomy—as one psychologist has expressed it, "for a freedom from restraints that bespeaks an inner rebelliousness and a fearlessness in the face of risk."[17] Lyle M. Spencer of McBer concurs: "The entrepreneur is the wild man in an organization. He pushes the rules to the breaking point. He hungers for a free range; he feels stifled in any organization except his own."

These qualities do not serve the entrepreneur well in corporate life. Most successful entrepreneurs have had short stints in larger organizations and profited, educationally, from the experience. But the friction they cause and the frustration they experience are too great for them to stay long. So common is this pattern that one consulting firm has coined yet another label—*exitpreneur*—to describe those who use brief organizational experiences as training to start their own businesses. According to the New York firm BeamPines, an "exitpreneur" is:

- Frustrated by corporate structure
- One who loves work; everything else comes second, including family
- Driven by fear of failure and a tremendous sense of urgency
- Willing to forgo the trappings of corporate power, posi-

tion, and security to achieve autonomy and be rid of red tape
- Motivated to create an organization where he or she is indispensable, and money is not a prime motivator
- A hands-on, opportunistic manager with an "I-can-do-it-better" attitude
- Totally committed and finds it hard to understand why others might be less committed
- Willing to risk losing life savings

The emergent picture of the entrepreneur is one of an individual who is uncomfortable in and even disdainful of traditional organizations. This suggests that even if an organization created a "skunkworks" or halfway house, there are likely to be few people in the organization of an entrepreneurial bent to take advantage of it. Moreover, entrepreneurs who are in organizations are likely to be short-timers, there to learn as much as possible as quickly as possible, and then get out on their own. True entrepreneurs are likely to see any organizational links, however ephemeral, as constraints, limits on their autonomy; they are not fooled by the chance to be *intra*preneurs. Entrepreneurial man is not organizational man and vice versa. Nor can one be made into the other by manipulating organizational structures, controls, and procedures: they are fundamentally different breeds!

The "myth of entrepreneurial management" has a magic all its own. There is something captivating about the image of the little guy with a good idea who risks all he has, gives all he has, goes against the giants and wins. It taps into America's love of the new and the underdog, all wrapped into one. However, as an approach to management, entrepreneurial practices may be more mirage than miracle.

There are two assumptions/myths that must be exposed about entrepreneurial management. The first myth is that entrepreneurial management is more efficient, effective, and innovative than management as practiced in larger, more traditional organizations. Many entrepreneurial firms are efficient, effective, and innovative; *most* are not—witness the failure rate of small businesses. It is the case that successful entrepreneurial organizations—small, autonomous, participative concerns—enjoy high quality, high productivity, and committed, creative workers. From such observations comes the belief that all organizations ought to emulate entrepreneurs. Enter the second myth. It is not the case that making organizations smaller, decentralized, and more participative will imbue them with the benefits of entrepreneurial organizations any more than it is true that putting an organization man in an entrepreneurial setting will make him an entrepreneur.

The myth of entrepreneurial management is that the benefits popularly associated with downsized, decentralized, participative, entrepreneurial management *may not exist*. To the extent that the promised entrepreneurial behaviors do exist, they are the product of certain specific conditions that may or may not be present for all managers in all organizations. Managing without the myth of entrepreneurial management means eschewing automatic adoption of all that is entrepreneurial and, instead, *choosing* those elements of structure, decision making, involvement, and innovation that are most appropriate for a particular organization at a particular time. This will mean, at times, going against the trend to downsize or decentralize, or whatever the management of the moment may be. When all around you are "getting small," it takes managerial leadership to forgo rhetoric in favor of reasoned reflection. Unfortunately, popular models of leadership seem to promote rhetoric over reason, and managers up and down the line harken to their messiahs.

5

The Myths of Messianic and Managerial Leadership

CEO: Command Entertainments Officer
CEO: Customs Enforcement Officer
CEO: Casualty Evacuation Officer
—Acronyms, Initialisms & Abbreviations Dictionary
(1986–87)

Business leaders today are more visible and more vocal than ever before. Even the most disinterested of observers of the corporate scene cannot escape knowing something of the near-legendary exploits of Lee Iacocca, Ted Turner, Steven Jobs, Mary Kay Ash, H. Ross Perot, Victor Kiam, Malcolm Forbes, T. Boone Pickens, and Donald Trump, to mention only a few. The country is rapidly approaching the day envisioned by Lester B. Korn, chairman of Korn/Ferry International, when CEOs are household words: "I expect to see the day when just as most Americans can name ten or fifteen major entertainers and ten or fifteen major athletes, they can name an equal number of corporate executives." The current interest in CEOs borders on obsession, an obsession fed by best-selling business biographies. We know where the celebrity CEOs buy their suits, what they have for breakfast (Hicks Waldron, CEO of Avon Products, has cornflakes, orange juice, one piece of toast, and decaffeinated coffee every day), and the average length of the average CEO's work day (up at 5:49 A.M., at the office by eight, home at 5:52 P.M.). For all that our fascination with celebrity CEOs has uncovered interesting tidbits about their lives, it has revealed little about their leadership, about *how* they lead. Looking at celebrity CEOs, H. J. Zoffer, dean of the University of Pittsburgh's Graduate School of Business, has defined leadership as "a charismatic, almost messianic quality that, through the judicious use of power and forceful and dramatic postures, somehow inspires the loyalty of followers and galvanizes attention on the leader and his projects."[1]

The message from celebrity CEOs to managers who would be leaders is "Be messianic." Those managers who have difficulty seeing themselves as deliverers have an alternative model of leadership: "managerial leadership." Managerial leadership is the product of the over 4,000 empirical studies on leadership conducted in the last century, two-thirds of which have been conducted in the last twenty-five years. These studies have established a wide range of variables that affect leadership, everything from the physical attributes of the leader to legal and political influences on the organization. Managerial leadership argues for the mastery of these influences through learned techniques of efficiency and effectiveness: "accomplishing goals efficiently, cost-effectively and imaginatively, while respecting the lives and welfare of subordinates and advancing the welfare of the broader community."[2]

The apparent contradictions between messianic and managerial mask the fundamental leadership issues: (1) close examination proves *both* models to be mythical, and (2) contemporary experience raises important questions about how much any manager *can* or *should* lead. These issues suggest significant changes in the ways organizations and managers think about leadership.

The messianic model of leadership has a rich historical tradition. At the turn of the century, the German sociologist Max Weber described the religious prophet as the prototype of charismatic leadership—a person with extraordinary powers over others simply by virtue of natural endowment. If business be the religion of our times (and there are many who argue persuasively that it is), CEOs are the messiahs made so by their charisma. Among these prophets, Lee Iacocca is the high priest—the charismatic leader with the most charisma.

Lee Iacocca emerged from the ranks of faceless managers to

change the fortunes of the giant Chrysler Corporation. That done (with the help of friends above him—the U.S. government; and below him—the UAW), he turned his attention to re-igniting the spirit of America, both figuratively and literally, with his leadership of the program to restore the Statue of Liberty. His autobiography led the best-seller lists for two straight years, selling nearly three million copies. In those same years, Iacocca ranked among the Gallup Poll's "Ten Most Admired Men in America"— the first businessman to make the list since Bernard M. Baruch in 1958. The ultimate testimony to Iacocca's superstar status may have been his cameo appearance on the hit TV show "Miami Vice" in 1986.

Iacocca is the epitome of the charismatic, celebrity CEO, but he is not alone. Countless others have written biographies highlighting their business acumen. And it's not just in books that CEOs have sought to establish themselves as public personae. In recent years, company leaders have increasingly taken to appearing in print and electronic media campaigns as spokespersons for their products. Some business leaders are so recognizable that they are enlisted to do ads for other products, much as movie stars or athletes are used in testimonials.

The CEO as biographer and as spokesperson is all part of the CEO as celebrity—a status to which many business leaders aspire today. Few have been as unabashed in their seeking of celebrity status as Victor K. Kiam, best known for his television commercial in which he claims, "I was so impressed with the Remington Shaver that I bought the company." Apparently Kiam was so impressed with his own leadership that he printed on the jacket flap of his book *Going for It!* a signed statement proclaiming, "I am so confident that you will benefit from and enjoy this book that if you are not satisfied, I will give you your money back." As if that was not enough, Kiam spent more than $1 million of his own money on radio and television advertising for his book. Kiam, while promoting his book, was also trying to raise money for a TV game show that would have entrepreneurs contesting for a $100,000 prize, with himself as the host/emcee, of course.

Rarely is money the motivation for these self-promotional efforts, as Kiam's free spending attests. Many times the celebrity CEOs do not even keep their royalties, but instead pledge them to charitable concerns. The dominant motives seem to be fame, reputation, even competition, and, in some cases, revenge (witness Iacocca's railing against Henry Ford II). Vanity seems to be the common denominator. Most CEOs, though reluctant to admit it, would like to bask in celebrity and be seen by others as they see themselves, as the central player in a business drama— as a modern-day messiah. The celebrity CEOs (and their ghostwriters) seem primarily intent on writing themselves into a place in business history. Yet, to a man (few women executives have promoted themselves as messianic leaders, the exceptions being Mary Kay Ash, Estee Lauder, and Sydney Biddle Barrows), they vow that their purpose is to tell their story so others may learn from their experiences. And millions have turned to these messianic business leaders for learning.

It is perfectly natural in an era of economic uncertainty to look to business leaders as messiahs. Instability produces stress for institutions and individuals alike. People have always looked to messiahs in such times, in hopes of deliverance from chaos. In successful businessmen and businesswomen, we see affirmation of the American dream and our own aspirations; by identification and projection, we can absorb some of their achievement and feel better about ourselves. But can we learn anything from the model of messianic leadership about how to become a leader? What to do as a leader? How to develop leadership in others? Probably not.

The leadership lesson from the messianic model can be summed up in the simple dictum, "Be messianic!" From the messiah figures themselves we get clichés. Iacocca advises: Be decisive ("use committees but bring them to a decision"). Listen ("take Dale Carnegie courses"). Be in the trenches. Do not "strategize endlessly."[3] From T. Boone Pickens comes the wisdom: "Master the art of leadership. Concentrate on goals. Forget about age. Keep things informal. Keep communication lines open. Play by the rules. Hire the best. Keep fit. Enjoy it."[4] Mary Kay Ash advises leading by "the Golden Rule."[5]

Most "scientific" studies of celebrity CEOs are scarcely more informative. Professors Harry Levison and Stuart Rosenthal interviewed the CEOs of six of the country's leading corporations: Citicorp, IBM, GE, the New York Times Company, Monsanto, and AMAX Inc. They came up with this composite of characteristics of business leaders. "The leader (1) is able to take charge; (2) has a strong self-image and a powerful ego ideal; (3) interacts with customers, employees, and other constituencies supportively; (4) provides permission to take risks; (5) is a thinker as well as a doer."[6] Business writer Charles Garfield researched over 1,500 peak performers—leaders in their chosen fields—and came up with six common attributes: (1) a strong sense of mission; (2) well-defined goals; (3) a capacity for self-observation and self-analysis; (4) the ability to bring out the best in others; (5) the mental agility to steer a "critical path" through complex situations; (6) the foresight to anticipate and adapt to major changes without losing momentum.[7] Finally, Roy Rowan of *Fortune* magazine cut through to the core of contemporary business leadership, reducing traits and characteristics to *the* key element: "It's intuition—the ability to play hunches, to sift facts and act decisively without conscious rational thought."[8]

These descriptions of the qualities of business leaders say little more than a leader is a leader because he leads and he leads because it is his nature to do so. Messiahs behave messianically. The point is not that such descriptors are inaccurate; leaders *do* lead, but knowing that, we know nothing more about *how* they lead or how to prepare others to lead. The lesson of messianic leadership is meaningless to managers; it may also be dangerously misleading.

To begin with, there is reason for healthy cynicism regarding the degree to which prominent business personalities are truly the leadership force behind business successes. John Kenneth Galbraith has observed the exaggerated role given to personality in the exercise of leadership—in part due to historical precedence (the great leaders of the past), in part due to vanity, and in part due to the synthetic, or created, personality: "Personality, as noted, reflects an earlier and more primitive stage in the exercise of power; thus it appeals to the archaic instinct that controls much of the comment on these matters. It is also more interesting than organization. And far more readily than organization, it appeals to the reporters, television commentators, and others who deal with the exercise of power and who associate it with what speaks, walks, and is seen. As a highly practical matter, people can give interviews and appear on television; organizations cannot."[9]

Galbraith suggests that what is presented to the public as inspirational leadership may be illusory. The belief that leadership is intuition and inspiration promotes a grand illusion in leadership, an illusion with dire consequences for leaders and followers alike—the Illusion of Greatness. This leads executives and managers to believe that if they are seen as great (present the illusion of greatness), they will be great; and it leads these same executives and managers to believe their own publicity, to think of themselves as great.

The self-promotional efforts of executives such as James L. Dutt, Donald Trump, William Farley, and thousands of others waging similar, if less visible, campaigns in thousands of companies, using everything from lavish life-styles to naming products after members of their family, can, at one level, be dismissed as mere egocentrism. Their privileges of rank, lamentable to be sure, are a little bit laughable at the same time. Unfortunately, these would-be messianic leaders are simply doing what they, and most of their followers, feel needs to be done—they are presenting/packaging themselves as leaders. If the occasion to be a messiah doesn't arise (as it rarely does) in the normal course of enterprise, the next best thing is to appear to be messianic—to manage one's image in such a way that one is perceived by employees and the public as an intuitive and inspirational leader. Supervisors, foremen, management trainees, junior executives, middle managers, and vice-presidents spend more time and effort *trying to be seen as leaders* than they do leading. Most things managers do to *present* themselves as leaders—the politicking, posturing, personal packaging, and self-promotion—actually distance them from work and workers, the very arena where they have to *prove* themselves as leaders. In a sense, many managers are like young people who want to be rock stars. They don't want to play music well. They don't want to compose music. They just want to be rock stars. The illusion of greatness does the same thing to would-be leaders. Many managers today have no interest in leading well—they just want to be seen as leaders. This motivation often leads to comical results, especially when junior executives cloak themselves in the garb of messianic leaders. But it is not comical for those who are managed by aspiring celebrity leaders.

A more invidious consequence of the messianic model of leadership is a second-order outcome of the illusion of greatness—the "leader" begins to think of himself as great. Kenneth E. Clark, former director of the Center for Creative Leadership, has observed this danger: "Any CEO begins to have more feelings of confidence in his plans than he deserves. After a while you think you're something special. You think you can handle every problem and you can't. That's worse among celebrity executives."[10] The real problems begin for celebrity executives when they fall victim to the illusion of greatness they have created—when they begin to believe their own press releases. Being taken in by their own illusion seems to be a particular sin for young executives, perhaps because they are unsure of the legitimacy of their leadership.

Bobby Sakowitz, fourth-generation chairman who guided the family-owned and -named retailer from its 1982 peak of seventeen stores and $130 million in sales to a Chapter 11 reorganization in 1985, was victimized by his own illusion. The dashing Sakowitz, fond of a high profile, exotic travel, blue-ribbon civic committees, and being an item in the gossip columns, was also fond of making every decision himself—from the color of the stores' carpeting to which couture lines to buy. Jerard L. Less, president of Colton Bernard Inc., a New York apparel consulting firm, said: "He committed the oldest sin of a family business. He wanted to do everything himself."

Young CEOs and would-be heroic leaders are not the only ones to fall victim to their own illusions. Consider the tumultuous tenure of James L. Dutt, former chairman (1979–85) of the $12.6-billion multinational food and consumer goods giant, Beatrice Companies. Dutt became chairman of Beatrice in 1979. At the time, the company was a loose confederation of mostly regional food companies. Dutt brought to his job a vision of Beatrice as a worldwide market leader in food and consumer products—a household word. He also brought some strong views about what to do and how to do it and a low tolerance for those who disagreed with him. For example, Dutt launched a $30-million corporate image advertising campaign, "We're Beatrice," which insiders and industry analysts suggested was of questionable benefit other than to glorify Dutt. In addition to requiring that his picture be hung in every Beatrice office, he refocused the corporate magazine and other publications to emphasize his exploits. An avid car collector and racing enthusiast, Dutt committed an estimated $70 million to sponsor a Formula I racing team *after* he had sold off STP, Beatrice's only automotive product line. He pushed for the $2.7-billion acquisition of Esmark Inc. at twenty-three times earnings. How could one man, even at the top, have led such a huge corporation to go so wrong? The answer lies in a fundamental vulnerability of heroic leadership— "groupthink."

In 1972, Irving L. Janis coined the term *groupthink* to refer to "a mode of thinking that people engage in when they are deeply involved in a cohesive in-group, when the members' striving for unanimity overrides their motivation to realistically appraise courses of action."[11] Janis's analysis saw groupthink at work on the national level in the lack of defense of Pearl Harbor (1941), the invasions of North Korea (1950) and the Bay of Pigs (1961), and the escalation of the Vietnam War (1964–67). Watergate (1974) and the trading of arms to Iran for hostages (1986) could be added to the list as well. A necessary precondition for group-think is the presence of a strong (charismatic), directive leader whose approval/acceptance is sought by group members, so much so that they avoid criticism and sacrifice their own judgment in pursuit of the leader's favor and the group's cohesiveness. Galbraith has termed this same process the "sycophantic effect."[12]

The conformity-seeking tendency of the group surrounding a messianic leader is heightened when the strong leadership occurs in a complex and dynamic environment where there is high stress on decision makers, and the group is relatively insulated from outsiders. Groupthink is not demonstrated only by evidence (albeit hindsight) of a poor decision. The telltale marks of group-think are certain processes: (1) the illusion of invulnerability; (2) collective rationalizations; (3) belief in the inherent morality of the in-group; (4) stereotyping the opposition; (5) pressure on doubters and dissenters; (6) self-censorship of misgivings and doubts; (7) illusion of unanimity; (8) mindguards to protect the group from adverse information.

Groupthink was much in evidence at Beatrice under Dutt. During his tenure at the top, over three-quarters of the top sixty officers in the company left or were fired. He increasingly isolated himself from the rest of management, putting a former secretary in as his personal chief of staff. He frequently retreated into seclusion. Ultimately, his decision-making style and his decisions led to his ouster, leading insiders and outsiders to observe that he may have done a lot for himself but he didn't do much for Beatrice. One executive who left Beatrice in the wake of Dutt's takeover suggested this obituary for Dutt: "It's as if he became possessed. He [thought he] was the only one who could run the company."[13]

Rarely are corporate decisions chronicled in such a way as to give outsiders an insight into leader-decision processes. However, anyone reasonably conversant with the popular business press can generate a list of nominees from the manner in which some very visible and very questionable recent corporate decisions have been defended: Texas Instruments' disastrous foray into consumer products, especially watches and home computers, in the early 1980s; Mobil Oil's purchase of Montgomery Ward in 1974; the introduction of New Coke in 1984; the E. F. Hutton check overdraft scheme of 1985; the 1986 GM buyout of Ross Perot; the United Airlines Inc. change to Allegis Corporation in 1987. Bad decisions are not in and of themselves evidence of groupthink; ignorance and simple error may be the cause. But messiah-dominated decision processes are vulnerable to distortions, and the rigorous defense of such decisions frequently points to the effects of groupthink.

Even those corporate leaders who do embody the intuition and inspiration of messiahs, whose greatness is not illusory but instead factual, are not without fault. They manifest yet another failing of the messiah model, the problem of succession. After all, how do you follow a messiahlike leader? During the tenure of a celebrity CEO, all of the internal energy of the organization is focused on and around him and his image. Little or no attention is given to grooming a successor; understandably so, since the conventional wisdom of messianic leadership believes that when the occasion demands it, a leader will arise. However, it is rare that one messianic leader is immediately followed by the ascension of another. The departure of a messianic leader typically leaves a leadership vacuum. Once a successor has been appointed/anointed, he usually finds it difficult, if not impossible, to follow a legend. Gulf + Western Inc. has had a difficult time managing its diverse portfolio since the death of Charles Bluhdorn in 1982. Edwin Land, founder and CEO at Polaroid, left a void that took Israel MacAlister Booth five years to fill. CBS Inc. lacked direction in the years immediately following the retirement of William S. Paley. Who can hope to be a successful successor to Armand Hammer at Occidental Petroleum Corporation? To Iacocca at Chrysler? To Ted Turner? So long as these leaders are perceived to be successful because of who they are, masters of the messianic qualities of intuition and inspiration, their successors cannot be developed—they simply must be.

Sadly, it seems that the lesson to be learned from the messianic model of leadership and from the biographies of messiah leaders is that leadership cannot be learned. There is no doubt that there are messianic leaders. Throughout time and history, intuitive, inspirational individuals have emerged in times of crisis; they have turned the tide of events and the fortunes of their fellow man. But rarely can we learn from these messiahs their mystique, how to do what they do. It is a myth to suggest to managers that they can lead by being messianic. What is the message to those managers who are not by nature intuitive or inspirational yet still aspire to leadership? What does the messianic message portend for those who are in leadership positions and wonder how to perform? What should the organization that needs to develop leaders from within its ranks do? Must we hope for leaders to be born or can they be made? Is leadership mystique or technique? The managerial model of leadership argues that every man(ager) can be a leader—intellect can substitute for intuition and inspiration.

Most of the voluminous body of research on leadership represents perfect examples of what was described in Chapter 2 as the failure of science to speak to the problems of managers. Incomprehensible treatises on inconsequential elements dot the landscape of leadership literature: "Leader-Member Agreement: A Vertical Dyad Linkage Approach"; "Toward Reciprocal Determinism in Leadership Theory"; "Theoretical, Information Processing, and Situational Factors Affecting Attribution Theory Models of Organizational Behavior"; and so on. These are a far cry from Iacocca's formula for success, or the six qualities of peak performers, or the simple dictum to "Be intuitive and inspirational." There are also a large number of incestuous investigations in the leadership literature—studies of studies little known to anyone in a position of leadership but coded with passwords to those who theorize about leadership: the Vroom-Yetton model, the Hi-Hi Style, Fiedler's model, and a host of others. There is, in short, a language of leadership spoken by a select few to a select few. The question for managers is: Are they saying anything important? Anything that managers can use? Probably not.

What they are saying is that you don't have to be a messiah to lead; you can instead master elements of the leadership situation, elements which include:[14]

- *Characteristics of the Leader*
  Traits
  Skills
  Competencies
  Physical attributes

- *Behavior of the Leader*
  Informing
  Consulting and delegating
  Problem solving and crisis management
  Clarifying roles and objectives
  Monitoring operations
  Motivating task commitment
  Recognizing and rewarding
  Supporting
  Developing
  Harmonizing and team building
  Representing
  Interfacing

- *Leader Power*
  Legitimate
  Expert
  Referent
  Reward
  Coercion

- *Intervening Variables*
  Subordinate characteristics
  Group characteristics
  Role characteristics
  External resources

- *Exogenous Situational Variables*
  Task-technology characteristics
  Organizational-legal-political factors

- *End-Result Variables*
  Productivity
  Effectiveness
  Psychological health
  Development and growth

No wonder we think of leaders as heroes! It takes a heroic effort just to understand the leadership maze. In the science of leadership, *everything* matters and what matters most is how everything is *managed*. In effect, what science has done is to redefine leadership, leadership as synonymous with management. Science has countered the heroic leader with the *managerial leader*—substituting technique for intuition.

If Lee Iacocca is the paragon of the heroic leader, Alfred Sloan is the managerial leader par excellence. Sloan told how he did it in his 1963 classic *My Years with General Motors,* which detailed his forty-five years of tenure with GM.[15] James O'Toole, management professor at the University of Southern California, attributes to Sloan the definitive expression of American managerial philosophy:

- First, he altered the value structure of big business: he promoted efficiency over creativity and risk-taking as the key attribute of large, publicly held corporations.
- Second, he erected a wall between the world of the entrepreneur and the world of the professional manager that has not since been breached.
- Third, he developed a classic system and structure for managing giant enterprises.
- Fourth, he bequeathed a legacy of "how-to's" that forms the principal body of knowledge of modern, corporate strategy, finance, accounting, marketing, and production management.[16]

Sloan was not one to "intuit and inspire"; his was an engineering perspective, not an emotional one; his vocabulary was *economizing, utility, facts, objectivity, rationality, maximizing.* Lest one wonder where Sloan stood on the subject of leadership, consider his observation on Billy Durant, the entrepreneur who founded GM: "Mr. Durant was a great man with a great weakness—he could create but not administer." In Sloan's eyes the leadership of large corporations required not creators but administrators.

No managerial leader present or past did more with the tools of his trade—reports—than did Harold S. Geneen, CEO at ITT from 1959 to 1977. Geneen's managerial philosophy is summed in the accountant's beatitude, "The drudgery of the numbers will make you free." Geneen made a religion of financial control. He spent untold hours personally reviewing the quarterly budgets of over 200 ITT managers worldwide. To Geneen budgets were "a series of expectations expressed in numbers" and "thermometers which measure the health and well-being of the enterprise."[17] Wickham Skinner, Harvard Business School professor, writing in the *Harvard Business Review*, said of Geneen:

> His successful years made him a model of modern scientific management. He rose to the top and brought about change and growth and outstanding financial performance by his use of numbers. As an assembler and analyst of numerical data, not only was he world class in imagination and competence, but he was also a leader of an entire generation of managers in the use of financial data for planning, budgeting, and control. The widespread adoption of the annual financial plan is partly the result of his impact on management. That is the way most companies are now managed.[18]

The real attraction of the concept of managerial leadership as epitomized by the likes of Sloan and Geneen is that it requires no particular native talents other than the ability to master certain techniques. The managerial leader, unlike the messianic leader, is not born but made—made from his or her mastery of the leadership techniques. These techniques have been embraced and embellished by business schools, seminar leaders, and management consultants who see in them not only the essence of leadership but the elements of an industry, leadership training and development. Managerial leadership accounts for the success of messianic leaders (good science must explain *all* cases) by explaining that different individuals have different ways of mastering the leadership techniques. The messianic leader is one style, one way to put together the techniques of managerial leadership. Geneen's "style" was to focus leadership techniques around controlling task behavior. Bob Frederick instituted a similar style when he took over from Thornton F. Bradshaw as CEO of RCA Corporation—requiring strategic planning and reports on every conceivable measurement of performance. Indeed, managerial leaders are far more prevalent than messianic leaders in organizations of every size and description. Managerial leadership with its attendant techniques is presented as the "professional" leadership today.

Popular and professional though it may be, managerial leadership is not without its pitfalls. Critics of managerial leadership are fond of saying, "Leaders are people who do the right thing and managers are people who do things right." The target of this attack is the "professional manager." University-trained, upwardly mobile, loyal to career rather than to a company, professional managers are the technocrats of today's management techniques. United Technologies Corporation of Hartford, Connecticut, took out a full-page ad in the *Wall Street Journal* in 1986 under the headline:

Let's Get Rid of Management

People don't want to be managed.
They want to be led.
Whoever heard of a world manager?
World leader, yes.
Educational leader.
Political leader.
Religious leader.
Scout leader.
Community leader.
Labor leader.
Business leader.
They lead.
They don't manage.
The carrot always wins over the stick.
Ask your horse.
You can *lead* your horse to water, but you can't *manage* him to drink.
If you want to manage somebody, manage yourself.
Do that well and you'll be ready to stop managing.
And start leading.

In a more reasoned commentary, Professor H. Edward Wrapp of the University of Chicago captures the complaints about professional managers with this summary: "In the mistaken belief that they can run any kind of business, they have helped inspire the current conglomerate binge. They have created false expectations and wasted untold numbers of dollars and man-hours by making a religion of formal long-range planning. They have lessened the ability of people to work together by overemphasizing specialization, and then wrought untold pain and havoc by seeking to solve all problems by means of reorganizations."[19]

In managerial leadership, management, specifically the *tools* of management, can take precedence over leadership; forms supersede function; process can come before purpose; measures before meaning. Critics of managerial leadership do not lack for examples of their concerns. Harold Geneen's style provides the purest example of managerial leadership at its best and at its worst. In 1974, after fifty-eight consecutive quarters of 10-percent-plus profit gains, ITT earnings declined. That was only the beginning of problems for the corporation; there followed sick divisions, divestitures, large write-offs, massive firings, quarrels with governments in Europe, and congressional exploration of the disaster in Chile, where ITT was accused of having conspired with the CIA to create economic chaos and revolution. This inquiry followed the prolonged accusations and hearings in which ITT was accused of using company funds to influence the settlement of antitrust action—the infamous Kleindienst–Dita Beard sessions over twenty-two days in 1972.

Robert J. Schoenberg in his biography of Geneen wrote: "The other side of the coin was a ruinous tendency to overprize management-by-the-numbers. The analysts, the accountants, the dealmakers, the lawyers, the controllers—all number crunchers—took over and no one was left to do any honest work. Production and the product were no longer glamorous. It was reason run amok, effacing the purpose of the enterprise."[20]

Geneen is not alone in his efficiency excesses. In every organization there are examples of processes put before purposes by managers more concerned with methods than with meaning. In the eyes of columnist Ellen Goodman, managerial leadership "is the modern management cult at its lowest common denominator. Read through the course catalog of an average business school. Sit through the local success seminar. You hear a whole lot more about process than about product.

"With all the fascination on how to manage, there is little taught about what to manage. And what not to manage. One of the concerns of American business is that the current class of mobile managers regards one company as interchangeable with another. It's more worrisome when we regard one goal as interchangeable with another."[21] As if illustrating Goodman's point, in a 1987 Associated Press story a Florida bank manager was reported to have embezzled $198,000, leaving behind a note detailing the "pros" and "cons" of his action and outlining a strategy. His decision-making technique was flawless.

Current efforts to address the critics of managerial leadership and put meaning back into management center on something called "visionary leadership." Donald M. Kendall, chairman of the board and CEO of PepsiCo Inc., has asserted that vision is the essence of leadership. "I believe the most important job of top management is to create a vision of the organization, a sense of purpose. And then to share that vision with others in the organization—so that everyone knows what it was that made the organization successful in the past and what it will take to ensure the continuation of that success. I think this is the essence of leadership—this sharing of the vision."[22]

When General Motors brought Electronic Data Systems into the already disparate GM family in 1984, Chairman Roger B. Smith saw to it that all of the new members of the corporate family received cards declaring the mission of GM: "The fundamental purpose of General Motors is to provide products and services of such quality that our customers will receive superior value, our employees and business partners will share in our success, and our stockholders will receive a sustained, superior return on their investment."[23] Smith's idea was that a clear articulation of this "vision" for the new GM would be a rallying point for employee efforts throughout the far-flung GM empire. Smith would not lead GM—the vision would lead GM.

Visionary leadership is a sort of middle ground between the polar positions of messianic and managerial leadership, an amalgam of mystique and technique. The notion of visionary leadership borrows from several popular management ideas. First, there is the concept of corporate culture: a vision is but a punchier statement of corporate goals or mission, and visionary leadership also draws upon the emotional commitment messianic leaders evoke from employees. Significantly, however, in visionary leadership the leader need not be particularly charismatic (we can't all be messiahs); the visionary leader asks not for personal allegiance but allegiance to a vision. Finally, visionary leadership embraces the role of the managerial leader inasmuch as the vision must be woven into the processes of the organization, typically through standard management techniques. For example, Warren Bennis and Burt Nanus of the University of Southern California have identified four common techniques among successful leaders: (1) *manage attention* through having a compelling vision; (2) *manage meaning* through communicating the vision and aligning individuals' interests and actions with that vision; (3) *manage trust* through reliability or constancy; (4) *manage self* through appropriate deployment of the leader's own resources.[24]

Visionary leadership does seem to have it all, but it doesn't have much that is new. For all of its attempt to be state of the art, this visionary or "transforming leadership" (so called because it alters the response of others) has a ring of familiarity about it. Over thirty years ago, the eminent management scholar Philip Selznick conducted a landmark leadership study and concluded that an effective leader "is primarily an expert in the promotion and protection of values."[25] Messianic leaders certainly promote values (even if nothing more than the value of their own leadership) and protect those values through the power of their personae. Managerial leaders promote and protect values through their control processes—*what* they count, *how* they count communicates what is important. Visionary leadership seems little more than a means for noncharismatic (some would say dull) leaders to evoke the emotional attachment commonly afforded messiahs—a means to every man as Iacocca. Inasmuch as there are not many messianic leaders in management, this may be an estimable contribution in and of itself. But it hardly deserves to be heralded as "new" leadership.

What strikes even the casual observer is that there is no difference between the old leadership and the new leadership. After all the attention over all of recorded history to discover who the leaders are and how they lead, we know little more than when we started. After 4,000 empirical investigations of every imaginable question about leaders and leadership, we have very few answers. Our original questions remain: Who are the leaders? How do they lead?

Maybe it doesn't matter. There is no doubt that leaders *can* matter. By virtue of their position in the organization and the opportunities that position affords them, leaders ostensibly *can* affect the values of employees. This can alter how employees respond to situations and thereby alter organizational performance. Whether a leader has the capability to act on these opportunities is largely a function of his or her talents and techniques. But how many opportunities does a leader *really* have to influence others? What is the strength of the leader's influence vis-à-vis other forces in and out of the organization? These considerations raise fundamental questions about just how much leaders matter.

To begin with, the success of any business enterprise is, to a large degree, determined by external forces over which the leader has little or no direct control. A ready example is the oil industry, where every economic actor, regardless of size, from the wellhead operator to the gasoline service station pumper, has his or her economic future tied to the price of oil, which in turn is determined by a handful of oil-rich countries. Companies, be they small oil field service companies or multinational mega-firms, can experience feast or famine, success or failure, and there is not a thing an individual leader can do about it. Supplies, markets, government regulations, the stock market, interest rates, the weather, demographics—the list of external forces that determine the fate of any enterprise is seemingly endless, and nearly all of the entries on the list are impervious to influence by organization leaders of any ilk.

Some have argued that it is the realization of the many distant, uncontrollable, and inexorable forces affecting organizational outcomes that underlie the exaggerated importance we attach to leadership. The belief that leaders cause success or failure is an extension of our need to believe that we can control our fate—if through no other mechanism than the selection and removal of leaders.

Often external events provide business executives with the opportunity to respond as leaders. These reactive situations maintain the legend of leadership. Johnson & Johnson had no way to plan for or to dissuade the fiends who laced Tylenol capsules with cyanide. The tragedy was an uncontrollable external event that could have ruined the company. Instead, Johnson & Johnson executives responded to the crisis with a display of responsible leadership, which restored the faith of the consumer and helped the company to regain market share quickly. Crises test the mettle of leaders, but they do so because they illustrate the essential vulnerability of organizations to elements beyond their control.

The same is true on the upside of the curve. External events can often put an organization in the right place at the right time through absolutely no effort by the leader at all.

At Volcanoes National Park in Hawaii, a helicopter service flies a regular schedule of sightseeing trips over Kilauea crater on Mauna Loa. Tourists are advised that once airborne, should the volcano begin to erupt, the price automatically doubles in mid-air. The spectacular lava flows late in the year made 1986 one of the tour service's banner years. As one manager observed, "Whether we have a good year or not is completely up to the volcano; we have nothing to do with it." Few businesses are made successful by active volcanoes, but just as external events can render the best efforts of leaders inadequate, they can also conspire to make lackluster leadership seem inspired. The Tax Reform Act of 1986 breathed new life into hundreds of struggling small accounting firms. The spread of AIDS in the mid-1980s resurrected a moribund condom industry. The trend toward drug testing of employees has spawned a new market for pharmaceutical concerns. The success stories here are not examples of enlightened visionary leadership (though company executives would have us think otherwise). They are merely more evidence that much of what accounts for organizational success (or failure) has little or nothing to do with leadership. It's "completely up to the volcano."

Even when external forces are neutralized, the influence of the leader may not be enhanced. Within organizations there are typically severe limitations on the opportunities and behaviors that leaders are allowed. In one research study, 2,123 managers, distributed across top, middle, and lower levels, were asked, "How much say or influence do you have in determining the work goals in the departments in the plant?" On a one-to-five response scale, the mean response was slightly less than three, the equivalent of "Some Influence"—hardly auspicious for the exercise of strong leadership. If top management is excluded, the mean perceived influence of middle- and lower-level managers drops down to "Very Little." These findings underscore the observation that, outside of the executive suite, opportunities to truly "lead" are few and far between; middle managers and junior executives might better invest themselves in learning "followship" rather than "leadership."

Given the rare organizational opportunity to exercise leadership, many managers find that their organizations dictate *how* leadership will be exercised. Most organizations have "organized out" leadership through policies, procedures, committees, task forces, and a variety of other means. These structural mechanisms are vigorously defended on the one hand as necessary controls (policies and procedures) and on the other hand as means to broaden participation in management. Both practices serve to dilute leadership. Policies and procedures do so by eliminating discretionary decision making. More than one manager has complained, "If they gave me formal authority commensurate with my responsibility, I could get the job done, but instead they tie my hands with rules and regulations." Participative practices dilute leadership by diffusing responsibility. When everything is done by groups and committees, it is difficult to determine who to credit or who to blame. It is difficult to determine who is a leader because the structures don't promote leadership. One senior oil company executive has complained of his company's leadership development program: "There's no sense developing leaders when we do everything by committee anyway. With everyone covering their ass by taking decisions into this group or that group, there's no way to figure out who's responsible for anything. As long as we're going to run the company this way, we don't need leaders; what we need are hostesses!"

In addition to organizing out opportunities for leadership, the norms, traditions, and training within companies about what is acceptable leader behavior further ensure that there will be minimum variation among managers; one leader will behave pretty much like the next. The larger the enterprise, the stronger the culture, and the fewer the opportunities for individualism in leadership. Ross Perot, during the days of his divorce from Roger Smith and GM, compared the leadership opportunities and behaviors in the company he founded, EDS, with those in GM: "At EDS when someone finds a snake, he gets rid of it. At GM when someone finds a snake, he calls in others to make sure that it's a snake. Then they call in an expert on snakes to consult with. Then they prepare a report on snakes." The inference is clear that the initiatives required for leadership aren't going to happen under the weight of GM structure and tradition. Large companies are not the only ones to constrain leadership. Some entrepreneurs set up rigid limits of authority and responsibility so that in their absence the business will be run as though they were there. Such practices do a lot for procedural consistency but they don't do much for the development of leadership.

Actually, few managers at any level in any organization have the opportunity to exercise leadership of the scale or significance imagined by the messianic school, the managerial school, or the visionaries. And, in those rare moments when the opportunity comes along, the would-be leader is likely to find that the direction has been predetermined, if not by policy or precedent then by his subordinates.

One of the most interesting findings to emerge from the research on leadership is the general discovery that, in small groups especially, followers have more influence on leaders than leaders do on the followers. This observation is particularly provocative when set alongside the noticeable absence of attention to followers in the celebrity CEO books of the messianic leaders. The managerial school acknowledges followers as a variable in the leadership equation but only as a target group on whom leadership is imposed, not as a group from which leadership flows. In fact, most current thinking about leadership has the process backward. Common sense tells us that it is the followers who make the leader. Unlike the philosophical cul-de-sac created by the question "If a tree falls in the forest and there's no one to hear it, does it make a sound?," we know that a leader is not a leader if there is no one around. But followers do more than make leaders, they make for the way leaders lead.

At a minimum, leaders are dependent upon the skill and motivation of their followers. No leader, however charismatic or managerially talented, can lead workers to do something that they do not have the knowledge or ability to do. And, without the use of physical coercion, a leader cannot make employees do things against their will. Thus, leadership in business requires a capable and compliant work force—employees who are able and willing to work.

Beyond this obvious dependency, there are many more subtle ways in which subordinates can influence their leaders and the leader behaviors they will respond to. For example, where the employees are "professionals"—scientists, engineers, lawyers, medical personnel—their work is usually more influenced by the standards and dictates of their profession than it is by their ostensible company leader. One senior manager of computer program designers describes his role: "I'd be kidding myself if I thought I could *lead* these people. They're pretty much free spirits. I sort of tell them where the boundaries are and then get out of their way. They're professional enough to know what needs to be done and how to do it." The ability, training, and knowledge of professionals together with the directives that come from the profession's norms and standards often create self-management that makes the role of the traditional leader trivial and redundant. Professional identification usually generates a high need for independence—they want to be left alone to do it their way—that can frustrate leadership.

The need for independence is not unique to professionals. Workers of unusual skill and ability, workers of long tenure, workers in very low-skilled, insignificant, "no-brains" jobs frequently feel that they can do it themselves and resist attempts to be led. Similarly, workers who, for whatever reason, are indifferent toward the rewards/punishments of the leader or those who feel as though the leader has no control over rewards/punishments are unlikely to be much influenced by leader behavior. In 1981, Magic Johnson, star guard of the Los Angeles Lakers professional basketball team, disapproved of the appointed leader, then-coach Paul Westhead. Johnson went directly to the owner, Jerry Buss. "I think as long as Westhead is the coach, I'm not going to feel like playing." Buss sided with his superstar and replaced Westhead with Pat Riley. Under Riley, Johnson and his teammates "allowed" themselves to be led to a championship. Union workers who perceive that the union exercises more control over their rewards and punishments than does their supervisor or even their company often show similar disdain for company leadership. Branch offices geographically removed from headquarters can be very cavalier about directives from on high. The regional manager for a national steakhouse franchise says of his attempt to lead the restaurant managers in his area: "It's pretty much an out-of-sight, out-of-mind thing with them. When I'm there I lead and when I'm not I don't. In fact, when I'm not there they do a lot of stuff I wouldn't approve of, but there's not much I can do about it from two hundred and fifty miles away."

Ability, experience, training, professionalism, routine jobs— all of these things can and do take the place of leadership. A need for independence, distance, indifference to the leader's control of rewards/punishments—all of these things can and do frustrate leadership even to the extent of neutralizing and even negating the influence of the leader(s).[26]

Many people in and out of the business community see corporate America in the throes of a leadership crisis. They point to the floundering economy, the burgeoning trade deficit, ethical scandals, factory closings, and a host of other symptoms of the crisis in leadership. Critics and supporters of business alike openly express concern over *who* the leaders are, *how* the leaders lead, and *where* the leaders are leading us. This attention to leaders and leadership is out of proportion to the real influence leaders exert on behavior. Leadership does matter but not nearly so much as the myth of leadership would have us believe. Opportunities for leadership and options for leader behavior are severely constrained by external forces, organization structures, policies, procedures, and by the behavior of those being led. Occasionally there are (a few) leaders who rise above the internal and external constraints to influence significantly the fortunes of their organizations and their followers. These messianic leaders cannot be made/developed and businesses cannot wait for them to be born. The messianic conception of leadership tempts managers to wrap themselves in the mantle of greatness, to be *seen* as messiahs, with potentially damaging results for organizations. The concept of managerial leadership offers methods for controlling and, thereby, influencing behavior but gives little meaning to those methods—spreadsheets don't lead.

If they discard these myths, what are managers left with? The answer is both less and more: *less* of an illusion of what leadership is, who leaders are, and how they lead; *more* of an understanding of the limits of leadership, *more* realism about the possibilities of leadership. Leaders are, and will continue to be, those who, by virtue of their person or position (and thereby control of organizational processes), influence behavior insofar as *they help others to meet their goals.* That is the real meaning of leadership: leaders help followers to get where *they*—the followers—want to go. This simple realization suggests a new way of thinking about leaders, leader behaviors, and leadership development.

"If you really want to be a leader, find out where the group is going and get in front of them." That advice, often given tongue-in-cheek, captures the essence of modern leadership. Effective leadership—helping people get to where they want to go—requires first, knowledge of where a group wants to go, and second, an ability to get in front of them by helping them get there. The leader as helper/servant is not myth— it is a recognition of the reality of modern-day leadership situations.

More often than not the members of a group or organization know where they want to go; they have a goal or objective in mind. All the leader needs to do to tap into this knowledge is to ask and to listen. At other times group members may have vague, differing, even conflicting views of the direction they ought to take. Here the leader's role is to act as a catalyst for clarifying the direction. Sometimes the leader can help followers discover where they want to go by presenting them with alternatives that capture their perspectives. This initial responsibility of the leader—finding out where the followers want to go—is also the leader's initial effort to help the group by focusing their energies and attention on a common goal. The leader must ask, listen, compromise, consolidate, clarify—skills seldom mentioned in the messianic or managerial models, where crowing and controlling are more the order of the day.

Once the leader has a sense of where the followers want to

go (perhaps has even helped to form it), he or she has to "get in front of them." How? By helping them get to where they want to go. Again, asking and listening are invaluable skills. "What can I do to help you? What resources do you need? What skills and abilities? What support?" Sometimes what is needed may be a sense of confidence that someone is in charge (messianic leader) or in control (managerial leader). At other times, followers may need additional resources, equipment, or training to get where they want to go. Or they may need nothing more than support for what they are already doing. Increasingly, there are and will be times when the help followers need and want is simply to be left alone so that they may do what they know how to do. In any case, to be truly helpful (and, therefore, to be truly a leader), the leader needs knowledge of what is needed, access to helping agents (resources, training, support), and the ability to make those helping agents available and useful to followers. In addition to being a good listener, the effective leader needs to be interpersonally capable—adept at building and maintaining mutually satisfying though ever-changing relationships—and to be able to teach. The effective leader also needs a supportive organizational context.

New perspectives on the leader's role suggest new leader-follower relationships, new leader skills, and a new organizational context for leaders—new selection strategies, new responsibilities, new development programs. Traditionally, organizations have looked to outstanding individual performers as the most promising candidates for leadership positions. The skills required to be a high individual achiever are usually quite different from those needed to *help others* get where they want to go. It should not be surprising that so few star performers turn out to be star leaders. Their talents are such that they themselves have not needed much help so they rarely understand the importance of helping. Moreover, they have been so focused on their own careers and competing with others that they have not learned helping skills. The members of an organization who have the highest potential for leadership are not those who have achieved the most themselves but, rather, those who have most helped others to achieve.

If leaders are to be helpers, they must be given the where-withal to be truly helpful. Organizations that have organized leadership opportunities out (via limiting policies and procedures and diluting practices) must organize helping back in. Leaders must be allowed discretion over the relevant helping resources—tangible (money, equipment, training) and intangible (support and encouragement)—that followers need to get where they want to go. Additionally, the organization must promote the model of leader as helper/servant by recognizing and rewarding helping behaviors. All too often corporate rhetoric proclaims servant leadership while practices prohibit leaders from truly helping and preclude recognition and reward of those who do.

Finally, companies must come to view leadership development in a new light if they want leaders to be helpers and servants. Not only must new development candidates be sought and new skills taught but leadership development must occur in a new context. Typical leadership development programs, be they in-company experiences or university- or consulting firm–sponsored management education, train just the leaders apart from the group they are to lead. Leadership is approached as something one learns in isolation and then one goes back and does it *to* followers. Such approaches actually diminish a leader's ability to help or to serve followers by suggesting that leader skills exist independent of followers and follower needs. Moreover, such approaches ignore the development of follower skills, i.e., how to get from leaders the information, resources, and support they need to do their jobs. Leadership development that separates leaders and followers develops neither the ability of the leader to help nor the ability of the followers to be helped. If they don't develop together, they don't develop at all.

Leadership is only one of a number of important managerial behaviors, even though it is commonplace today to write about leadership and management as though they are synonymous.

Discarding the myths of messianic and managerial leadership will alter some of the ways in which managers behave, but many myths will remain. One important myth has to do with how much responsibility managers have for the effort extended by employees and how managers exercise that responsibility. It is the "myth of the motivating manager."

6

The Myth of the
Motivating Manager

And as ye would that men should do to you, do ye
also to them likewise.
                                    —*Luke 6:31*

No matter how much you like vegetables yourself,
never try to feed a cat a carrot.
                                    —*Alex McEachern,*
                                    Organizational Illusions

Reports from every corporate quarter today suggest that worker
productivity, loyalty, and commitment are at all-time lows.
Managers cite declining productivity and quality figures and re-
cite lists of common employee behaviors that are at fault: habitual late arrivals and/or early departures; feigned illnesses and
unwarranted sick days; using company time and equipment to
operate other businesses; inordinately long lunch hours and coffee breaks; socializing with other employees; unwillingness to
learn new procedures. Estimates are that these and other employee practices cost American businesses up to $170 billion in
productivity each year. It is unquestionably a costly problem and
one that has managers everywhere concerned.

Managerial accusations of slackened productivity efforts are
largely affirmed by employees. In one survey, fewer than one in
four jobholders reported that he was working at his full potential. Nearly one-half of all workers said they put no more effort
into their work than what is required to hold on to their jobs.[1]
Clearly workers feel less than total commitment to their jobs.
Their defense is that they are only returning, in kind, the same

113

degree of loyalty that companies have shown them. The major mergers, takeovers, and cutbacks that have swept through industry after industry in the last decade have convinced workers that companies won't return their loyalty. Workers have learned that years of committed service mean little to an enterprise just getting by or to a new corporate parent eager for a quick turnaround. As a result, workers feel little compulsion to give the company their maximum effort; they do abuse company time and equipment; they are lax about quality; productivity drops and the cycle continues. Management reacts by cutting back or selling out.

Worker behavior is far from the only factor behind America's poor productivity performance over the last fifteen years. Problems of capital formation due to taxation, savings patterns, and a general redistribution of wealth; the effects of government regulation and legislation, especially in the areas of safety, pollution, employment, and energy; merger mania and the pursuit of paper profits; the changing composition of the work force and the values of new workers—all have contributed to the productivity problem. As important as these societal factors are, organizationally they offer few levers for change. There is little that any one company, much less a single manager, can do about these elements. Perhaps this is why so much attention is given today to worker motivation. Most managers recognize that they can do little to affect savings patterns, safety legislation, Wall Street profiteering, or worker values, but every manager feels he or she *can* or *should* influence worker motivation.

The belief that it is the manager's job to motivate employees is learned in business school and reinforced in managerial job descriptions. Popular business textbooks clarify the motivational role for students, who are prospective managers: "The achievement of the people who work with or for you is determined by three factors: (1) *motivation*, (2) *ability*, and (3) *resources*. You as a manager or co-worker have, in general, relatively little opportunity to increase people's ability or resources. What you have to work with therefore is motivation: a factor that is hardly ever at its maximum level and that can be greatly influenced by your actions. If you are ineffective in diagnosing causes of low motivation or in creating positive motivation, your presence will have little positive impact on the achievement of those around you."[2]

Managers accept it as their responsibility to inspire others to reach their full potential. If the potential of employees is not realized, it's management's fault for not motivating them. A survey of 236 top executives reported their nearly unanimous belief that "Management ineffectiveness is by far the single greatest cause of declining productivity in the United States."[3] Given the current condition of American business, this self-ascribed role of motivator has become something of a burden to managers.

In their search for the magical motivators, managers have looked far and wide but they have typically used a single lens, worker satisfaction. Management thinking about motivation has been largely based on the assumption that employee satisfaction causes employee performance, i.e., a happy worker is a productive worker. This assumption has led managers to some benign measures and to some bizarre measures in pursuit of the happy worker. In companies large and small, company picnics, Christmas parties, birthday cards, company softball and bowling teams, and employee appreciation days are still viewed by managers as important motivational measures. Such practices are the residual of an earlier time when paternalistic, womb-to-tomb management treated employees like family and received loyalty and commitment in return.

In an environment without layoffs, takeovers, and mergers, paternalistic practices did increase worker satisfaction (albeit short-term) and loyalty, although linkages between satisfaction and productivity have always been more difficult to establish. Today, however, the threat of layoffs is much more real for workers than company picnics or other paternalistic practices are rewarding. Noel Tichy, consultant and professor at the University of Michigan's graduate business school, notes: "Companies are now saying to their employees, 'We'll take care of you as long as we're winning.' That's a tremendous shift from the old paternalistic system."[4] Employee response to the "happy shop" has shifted accordingly.

Flagging corporate commitment, loyalty, and productivity are not isolated to the employee ranks; managers also show signs today of being less than fully motivated. Corporate instability has caused managers to shift their personal priorities—promotions and relocations are increasingly turned down in favor of family concerns. Other signs of managerial dissatisfaction are the record increases in absenteeism among salaried employees and the large number of senior managers taking advantage of early retirement packages. By the mid-1980s, less than 50 percent of managers rated corporate management favorably, twofold the percentage found disapproving in studies heretofore.[5]

Can the productivity problem be placed at the feet of managers, up and down the organization, who have not "satisfied" workers? Modern management mythology certainly thinks so. The only disagreement seems to be over what is needed to satisfy today's worker. Three approaches dominate current management thinking: individual motivation, group motivation, and organizational motivation.

In the lobby of Electronic Data Systems in Dallas, Texas, employees are greeted by two sculptures: one is a bust of Theodore Roosevelt, the other is a sculpture of an eagle rising into flight. Company literature describes the significance of these symbols: "The bust of Theodore Roosevelt is placed in the EDS lobby to remind us that it is the individual performer who deserves the credit, the employee who perseveres, who meets the demands of his job time and again with dedication and creativity. These are the individuals who have made EDS the company it is today." The message of the eagle is more succinct but similarly celebrates individual effort: "Eagles don't flock."

The philosophy of EDS embodies the spirit of America's oldest and most revered motivational system, the motivated individual.

Individual motivation systems rely upon a fundamental precept of human behavior: individuals will do those things for which they are rewarded. It is seen as both rational and right (fair, the American way) to reward individuals for their performance, and the greater the performance, the greater the reward; workers are not held back from being the best they can be and getting the most for their efforts. The operational principle of this system is to structure the work and/or reward system so that high performance is satisfying/rewarding to the worker. In this way, high performance leads to job satisfaction, and increased job satisfaction further spurs performance. All the manager has to do is put this perpetual motivational machine into action. To do this, managers can use either extrinsic rewards, such as pay and promotions, or intrinsic rewards, such as feedback, goal attainment, or an enriched job as a means to enhance individuals' job satisfaction and, presumably, their productivity. Motivation plans based on extrinsic rewards, whether pay, benefits, and/or promotions, can be thought of as pay-for-performance, whereas intrinsic reward-oriented motivation schemes are better thought of as praise-for-performance and performance-for-performance.

The purest form of individual motivation, pay-for-performance, is straight commission, long the standard compensation plan for salespeople in American businesses. In a straight commission plan, individual performance is measured by sales and the individual's pay is a percentage of sales. The more the salesperson sells, the greater the reward, hence, the greater motivation to sell. After some years of relative disfavor, pay-for-performance plans are returning to popularity. A survey of 600 companies by Hay Management Consultants found that over one-third are abandoning across-the-board increases or automatic cost-of-living adjustments in favor of pay-for-performance systems. At most megafirms this means introducing merit-based pay plans as a means of tying rewards of even nonsales personnel more directly to their performance. BankAmerica, for example, has introduced a system for rating its more than 86,000 employees in five performance levels. Employees in the top level receive raises at least 40 percent better than the bottom group, which is given a limited amount of time to improve performance or be let go. General Motors has put its 110,000 salaried staff members on pay-for-performance. TRW Inc., Honeywell, Hewlett-Packard, and a host of other major companies have similar, exclusively merit-based pay plans.

At smaller companies it is often easier to tie pay directly to performance without the complex and cumbersome (some would say capricious) merit reviews. Lincoln Electric Company, a Euclid, Ohio, manufacturer of welding machines, has had one of the most enduring pay-for-performance plans in American business. Since 1934, Lincoln workers have received roughly one-half of their annual pay in the form of year-end performance bonuses. Other pay-for-performance linkages get extra mileage out of the symbolic value of rewards. Ken Swanson owns and operates a $20-million construction company in California's Silicon Valley. On his desk sits a glass box containing a $10,000 Rolex watch. It is there to remind his seven project managers that anyone who brings in $500,000 in gross profits will get a watch. William A. Czapar, CEO of Anaheim Custom Extruders, goes a step further; he gets everyone in the family involved in boosting performance in pursuit of rewards. His managers and their wives know that if sales increase 30 percent, they all get a one-week, all-expenses-paid Caribbean cruise. "My goal was to get the wives involved. Then there's a little push from behind."

Research into operant conditioning has convinced managers that the immediacy of the behavior-reward linkage is an important element in motivation. This has led to even more immediate and direct pay-for-performance plans. At Ryan Transfer Corporation, a Wisconsin trucking company, every driver with more than one year's seniority gets paid a percentage of weekly revenues. Some pay-for-performance schemes are more elaborate. Every employee at Springfield Remanufacturing Center Corporation, from janitor to junior executive, has performance standards and incentive bonuses. Every month the company distributes to all of its 200-plus employees a detailed eighty-two-page financial statement so that each worker can measure his or her bonus. At Steelcase Inc., the Grand Rapids, Michigan, office furniture manufacturer, similar worker bonuses account for as much as 38 percent of annual compensation.

As fair and logical as it is, paying for performance can also be expensive. Wary of these money motivators, many managers have gravitated to individually oriented systems that do not rely on monetary incentives: praise-for-performance plans, so called because these plans assume that intrinsic rewards, such as managerial praise—in the form of feedback and recognition—are as rewarding and, therefore, motivating to employees as money.

Emery Air Freight has received a great deal of publicity for its behavior-modification program. Emery loses money if shipping containers are not fully loaded when shipped. Hence, a productivity goal is to ensure that empty container space is minimized. Before Emery's program was implemented, workers reported that they believed they were filling the containers about 90 percent of the time. However, a performance audit revealed that this was really so only about 45 percent of the time. In other words, over half of the containers were shipped unfilled. Through the use of feedback (in the form of self-report checklists provided to each worker) and positive reinforcement (praise from management), the percentage of full containers rose from 45 to 95 percent. Cost reductions for the first year alone exceeded $500,000, and rose to $2 million during the first three years. In other words, when workers were given constant feedback, kept informed of their performance, and praised, their output increased rapidly. As a result of this initial success, similar programs were initiated in other work areas at Emery, including the setting of performance standards for handling customer problems on the telephone and for accurately estimating the container sizes needed for shipment of lightweight packages.

In a similar application of goal-setting and feedback at Weyerhaeuser Company, the productivity of logging trucks was increased. Prior to the program the average net weight of loaded trucks had been about 60 percent of their maximum legal net weight. Management set a goal for loads to average 94 percent of maximum legal net weight. Drivers were given frequent feedback on their load weights and frequent reinforcement of the goal. Within three months the average net weight rose to slightly over 90 percent.

Another type of behavior-modification motivation program is in use at the Diamond International paper-egg-carton manufacturing plant in Palmer, Massachusetts. There, all 325 employees are allocated points in recognition of above-average performance. Any employee who works a full year without having an industrial accident is awarded twenty points; 100 percent attendance is worth twenty-five points. Every year, on the anniversary of the program's launch date, points are totaled up, and a record is sent to the individual's home. Upon reaching one hundred points, the worker gets a light-blue nylon jacket emblazoned with the company logo and a patch signifying membership in the One Hundred Club. Every one of the plant's employees has now earned a jacket. Additional gifts are available for employees who receive more than one hundred points. The program has been credited with productivity and quality improvements and betterment of labor-management relations.

Motivational programs such as those at Emery, Weyerhaeuser, and Diamond International are especially appealing to managers because in these instances there were no financial incentives for productivity improvement. They stand as "pure" examples of praise-for-performance leading to productivity improvements. The obvious attraction of behavior-modification and goal-setting programs, or the more popular variants management by objectives and the one-minute manager, is that the manager does not have to pay for performance with scarce dollars or equally scarce promotional positions. All the manager need do to motivate performance is provide employees with targets, give them feedback on how they are doing, and praise them when they achieve goals. In contrast to the limited extrinsic rewards, managers have an endless supply of information and praise (some would say because they rarely use them). What manager could resist performance improvements at such a reasonable price?

It is only a short step from praise-for-performance to performance-for-performance. Noting positive employee responses to challenging goals, many managers have aimed at increasing worker satisfaction (and therefore productivity) by giving them more responsibility, more variety, more significant tasks, and more identity with their task—in short, making the work more challenging. Managerial translation: you can get more out of workers if you give them more to do and, what's more, they'll like it! The assumption of job-enrichment/job-enlargement (JE) programs is that motivation lags because workers don't find work challenging. By increasing involvement with work itself, the results of work will increase.

A good example of the results of JE can be seen in the production of Rolls-Royces. Each RR grille, the distinctive marker of the car, is personally shaped, filled, and soldered by one of ten craftsmen in the Rolls grille shop at Crewe in Cheshire, England. On the back of each grille are letters stamped in the steel that denote the craftsman who produced it. The job has all of the elements of enrichment: responsibility—each worker is solely responsible for an entire grille; variety—several separate skills are required to produce a grille; significance and identity—each grilleman puts his personal stamp on his work. The results at Rolls-Royce are just what the JE supporters predict: motivation, pride, and productivity. When Tony Kent, a Rolls grilleman, made a company publicity tour of America, he visited the Carriage House Motor Cars showroom in New York City. Opening the hoods of several cars, he found one stamped with his mark. "This grille's mine," Tony said. "You can inspect it all you want but it looks perfect to me."[6]

American auto manufacturers have sought the same personal pride in performance with their own enrichment programs. At the Buick Product Engineering group, the job of assembler was enriched. Assemblers are skilled hourly mechanics who make experimental changes in fleet cars as directed by design engineers. When their jobs were enriched, assemblers were given further latitude to choose their own work assignments, inspect their own work, establish their own completion dates, and decide their job-hour content. The company has reported productivity increases, quality improvement, elimination of petty grievances, and a marked improvement in morale since implementation of the enrichment program.

Job enrichment/enlargement is not limited to assembly-line applications. Wherever job specialization is high and production/ service processes are routinized, job enrichment has been looked to as a means to resolve motivational problems. Chemical Bank in New York experimented with assigning clerks all of the duties of completely processing corporate accounts, from crediting payments to returning unsigned checks. Turnover was drastically reduced in the enriched clerical jobs. In one of the most often cited applications of JE, Travelers Insurance Companies enriched its keypunching jobs. Alerted to motivational problems by late and erroneous work and high absenteeism, management discovered that the keypunching and verifying jobs had extremely low motivating potential. They were not challenging—no skill variety, little task identity or significance, no autonomy, and low feedback. Jobs were redesigned by combining functions and building in client relationships and frequent feedback. The results of the Travelers job-enrichment program have been widely touted: the number of operators was reduced from ninety-eight to sixty, productivity improved nearly 40 percent, absenteeism declined 25 percent, and quality improved by nearly 10 percent. Management has estimated the cost savings at over $90,000 a year.[7]

Job enrichment has provided some dramatic productivity improvements but there have been problems as well. Most unions and many workers view JE as management's way of getting more without paying more. As evidence of management's real intent, they point to the number of instances in which job-enrichment programs have led to a reduction in the number of jobs. There is also a perplexing dichotomy in job enrichment. On the one hand, there are some jobs that even the most creative job engineers have concluded cannot be measurably enriched, hence, presumably the jobholders cannot be motivated. Yet even in these jobs one occasionally finds motivated workers. On the other hand, there are enriched jobs (most management jobs, for example) where workers are still not motivated. It may be that for many workers job content is not necessarily related to job satisfaction and/or to motivation. Giving workers (or managers) more to perform is not necessarily going to motivate them to perform more.

The costs of pay-for-performance, the complexities of behavior modification or praise-for-performance programs, and the limits of job enrichment notwithstanding, individual motivation systems still dominate current managerial thinking about motivation. Programs are continually introduced, altered, and ultimately retired only to be promoted again in revised form. This pursuit continues for two reasons: (1) the belief in rewarding individual performance runs deep in the American business psyche, and (2) the promise of increased performance without increased costs is simply too attractive for managers to cast aside. The logistical problems with the various individual motivation plans get most of the attention from managers who tweak at elements of the plans to fine-tune them to their company needs. This fine-tuning ignores a more fundamental problem with motivational schemes that link rewards to individual performance: performance itself is a hazy issue in most companies. How should performance be measured? What performance should be measured? How should performance be rewarded? The mythology of individual motivation suggests that managers can easily answer these questions; experience suggests otherwise.

The further a company moves its production process away from one worker producing one widget, the more difficult it becomes to measure both the quality and quantity of individual performance. It is relatively easy to measure the output of an individual who has complete control over the manufacturing process from raw resource to final product. But what if the final product depends upon the integrated efforts of many people? What if the worker is not involved in a product but rather a process like personnel or finance? White-collar productivity is particularly difficult to ascertain, raising the sticky motivational question, "How can you reward performances you can't measure?"

At Harris Trust & Savings Bank in Chicago, management has tried to deal with the slippery issue of white-collar productivity. A senior analyst on the project has described the task they confront: "It's easy to measure the output on the assembly lines—just count the number of bolts somebody puts into a car. But what's the output of a lawyer or an auditor? You can't just count how many audits or cases he handles because they are of all different types and of all different quality."

Efforts to measure white-collar productivity have historically not been very successful. The Bank of America identified seven activities in the loan officer's job. They then measured such things as the number of loans closed, the number of loans that became a problem, and the new accounts generated for other parts of the bank. A Chicago law firm tried to rank the cases lawyers handled by the degree of difficulty. Both the bank and the law firm eventually gave up their efforts, concluding such measurements were impractical. Measurement of scientific and creative performance has proven to be even more elusive. At Hughes Aircraft in California it was decided that the productivity of scientists couldn't be measured with a number. Hughes fell back on evaluations of such things as the backlog of problems, the number of errors, even "the degree of professionalism in getting the work done." The director of engineering-design management asserts that all that is needed "is a rough feel that things are going up or down." A "rough feel" is all that most companies have about individual performance of white-collar and professional employees. But a "rough feel" is a poor data base for tying rewards to performance, which is the essence of individual motivation programs.

In contrast to white-collar performance where work behaviors seem to defy measurement and most companies agree that a "rough feel" is as close as you can get, attempts to measure blue-collar productivity have taken on Orwellian overtones, thanks to computers. At Leprino Foods Company in Denver, on-board computers provide detailed information on each truck's trip: at what times it stopped and started, how fast the engine ran, how fast the truck was going throughout the trip. In a major insurance company, clerk-typists at terminals can be continuously monitored for keystrokes per minute. Supervisors of telephone operators can track how many calls each operator handles and how long each call takes. At Oxford Industries slacks factory in Monticello, Georgia, a computer monitoring system clocks every worker's pace to a thousandth of a second. The workers, mostly women, are paid according to how their pace compares with a factory standard for their job. An operator who beats the standard by 10 percent gets a 10 percent bonus over her base rate. If she lags 10 percent behind standard, she has 10 percent deducted from her wages. A terminal at every worker's station gives running updates of the worker's pace and wages.

These stringent performances solve one problem of pay-for-performance plans but are not always positive for workers or for the company. The National Institute of Occupational Safety and Health has cited computer monitoring as a possible reason for the high stress experienced by those monitored. Most affected unions have adopted official positions against monitoring; some have made it a contract issue. To date, seven states have considered legislation restricting computer monitoring of performance. It may not be necessary to legislate against computer monitoring of productivity; computer counting systems may carry the seeds of their own demise. In a program to monitor telephone operators at a utility company, whenever a caller had to wait over two minutes a loud buzzer would ring. The operators wanting to avoid the buzzer would answer calls with "Hello, I'm sorry I can't help you!"—then rush on to the next call. Callers didn't have to wait, but they didn't get the service they needed either. Customer complaints about poor service caused the company to drop its alarm system.

Faced with the difficulty of measuring many of the elements of performance that may be important to organizational goal attainment, managers often fall back on inflating the importance of those elements of performance that *can* be measured. The result is that rewards are tied to work behaviors that, at best, may have little or nothing to do with performance and, at worst, may be counterproductive, i.e., the telephone operators at the utility company. Measuring performance in order to reward workers may actually lead to paying for the wrong performance!

Ervin Schoenblum, consultant at Peat, Marwick, Mitchell & Company, observes, "If you start counting the wrong things, people will pump out what you measure, even if it isn't beneficial to the company. If a salesman is being measured on the number of phone calls he makes, for instance, he can call his girlfriend, bookies, and relatives, and never get any sales, yet by the measurement, he is doing fine."

Business professor Steven Kerr of the University of Southern California has termed this phenomenon "the folly of rewarding A, while hoping for B." It is a common pitfall of pay-for-performance programs. For example, insurance companies typically reward employees for the speed with which they handle claims. As pressure for production mounts, claims are settled with hurried, often careless review. High-volume performers are acclaimed for their production, but in racking up high clearance rates they may have given away the store. At a major airline, computer programmers were evaluated by the number of lines of code they wrote. As a result they wrote longer, looser programs rather than effectively minimizing commands. Kerr's research into goals and rewards asked, "What will most likely happen if you (a) set easy goals, then make them, and (b) set difficult, challenging goals, then miss some of them?" He found consensus response across industries and organization levels: missing difficult goals, even by narrow margins, is usually punished; making easy goals is rewarded. As an example, Kerr points out that most salesman in America are rewarded in proportion to the dollar volume of their sales. In very few firms is the difficulty of the sale taken into account. The "tough sale" is rewarded as any other. As a result, salesmen with territories like Beverly Hills and Scarsdale receive top commissions and annual readmittance to corporate America's "millionaires" and "Golden

Eagle" clubs, while salesmen assigned the poorer neighborhoods receive little pay and even less honor.[8]

In nearly every organization there are examples of rewarding A while hoping for B. Monthly sales quotas lead to salespeople "sandbagging" accounts. Once they've made quota for the month, they hold off processing additional sales until the next month, when it will count against a new quota. Managers measured on response time may build up excessive inventories to cut down dependence on delivery from their suppliers. Loan officers are encouraged to make loans and rewarded accordingly, whereas the desirable behavior might be for them not to make bad loans.

Individual performance-reward schemes get distorted in these ways because of managers' penchant for "objective" performance measurement criteria and the resulting overemphasis on highly visible/countable behaviors. The distortions so obvious to workers (who typically know the behaviors they need to perform and resent the fact that their every move is measured while managers are held accountable only to a "rough feel") emphasize how difficult it is to measure performance that really matters. Whatever can be measured is likely to be inflated in importance and may displace energy from what workers really ought to be doing—whether or not it can be counted.

Even when the appropriate performance can be measured, individual performance-reward motivation plans are left with the question "What is the proper relationship between pay and performance?" Is a $10,000 Rolex watch an appropriate incentive/reward for a project manager who brings in $500,000 in gross profit? Is the project manager the appropriate performer to reward? Should the workers who made the project manager successful similarly share a 2 percent reward on gross profit? It is a curious anomaly of American business that pay-for-performance is practiced mainly at the very top where it is often most difficult to assess individual productivity. Moreover, the measures of performance standardly used for executives—increases in gross profit, net profit, market share, etc.—are often determined by forces beyond the control of any individual manager.

These ambiguities result in some very curious pay-for-performance linkages. For example, during the recession years of 1981 to 1983, the average compensation of chief executives nearly doubled while national unemployment passed the 11 percent mark. General Motors asked the United Auto Workers for wage concessions at the same time that they announced record bonuses for management. In 1985, the earnings of E. F. Hutton Group had fallen 17.1 percent and investigations had revealed an illegal check overdrafting scheme, which reflected badly on management controls. How was this performance linked to pay? Robert Foman, head of E. F. Hutton, received a 23 percent raise to $1.2 million and was awarded 12,000 shares of stock. These are not isolated instances; in company after company throughout the 1980s, declining performance resulted in record pay packages for management. Rewards such as these at the executive level carry messages about motivation that speak much louder to employees than do elaborate systems for measuring insignificant behaviors.

These examples strike at the heart of the question of how much to pay for what. Should there be a consistent relationship between pay and performance, applied across the company, top to bottom? Should all the rewards go to the few highest performers? Should low performers be punished, have money taken away? Should *everyone* profit in the good times? Should *everyone* pay for the bad times? How can individuals be singled out for reward in a group or organization-wide performance? The way a company responds to these difficult questions often undermines everything it is trying to do with its pay-for-performance motivation philosophy and program. Demotivating practices can speak louder and longer than motivating philosophies.

The theory behind individual pay-for-performance motivation systems is sound: people do those things for which they are rewarded and avoid those things for which they are punished. The more the reward is perceived as attractive, the greater the effort people will make to do those things that are rewarded. It is also true that there are many rewards besides pay that are seen as attractive: recognition, advancement, autonomy, and challenge are all valued by employees. Experience with individual motivation plans has revealed the problems of (1) determining and measuring performance, (2) measuring and rewarding the wrong behaviors, (3) appropriately and consistently linking pay and performance, and (4) trying to reward without paying because paying for performance is expensive. Frustrated in their attempts to make individual motivation systems work, many companies and managers have turned to group-oriented motivation programs.

In addition to the difficulties making individual pay-for-performance plans work, two other forces have heightened managers' interest in group approaches to motivation. One is a growing recognition of the interconnectedness of job tasks. Due to the complexity of work, productivity is increasingly a group phenomenon; to improve group productivity, it is necessary to motivate the group. Also, companies have recognized that identification with a work group is a central element in an employee's relationship with an organization, and motivating the group is an important means to motivating individuals.

An Associated Press survey of American workers reported that next to the work itself, the one thing people liked most about their jobs was the people they worked with (32 percent and 23 percent respectively). The importance of this social dimension of work has long been recognized by the Japanese. It is their success with group participative methods, especially quality circles, that has reawakened American business to the potential of group motivation. As one owner observes, "People want to belong. They're either going to belong to unions or they're going to belong to churches, they're going to belong to something. . . . It's a basic human trait that goes through their fiber. You give them something to belong to and it goes a long way."

Not only do employees want to belong and value their work relationships, employees increasingly need to cooperate with one another in order to get their job done. Work "teams" are the product of a complex, interconnected work environment. For example, the nation's largest carrier of automobile insurance has discovered that effectively and efficiently serving the needs of policyholders requires the coordinated efforts of agents, underwriters, and claim handlers. The company has created cross-functional work teams that provide necessary coordination and a source of group identification for all involved. In another example at the executive level, Buford Television Inc., a small, innovative, Texas-based owner-operator of television and cable systems, created an acquisition team to implement its strategy of acquiring small cable systems. On the team are the key executives of every function needed to take a deal from inception through to takeover. These examples and, of course, the now nearly ubiquitous quality circles represent only the most recent attempts to tap into the performance potential of teams. Self-regulating work groups or teams have often been cited over the last twenty years as a largely untapped, powerful motivator.

In Europe, self-regulating production groups at Saab and Volvo have been operating for nearly twenty years. At the Volvo plant in Sweden, there is no assembly line. A new carrier was designed to transport an entire car around the plant to various work teams responsible for major parts of the assembly. Each work team has control over its work pace, inspections of work, and scheduling of its workers. The team members meet to resolve problems that come up. A similar organization has been in effect at Saab since 1969. In both companies the team concept is attributed with improvements in production, unplanned work stoppages, and employee attitudes and turnover. In this country, celebrated self-regulating work group programs at Alcoa's forged aluminum automobile wheel plant and at the Gaines Pet Food plant are credited with increased productivity, improved safety, lower turnover, and higher job satisfaction. For twenty years, the Gaines Pet Food plant in Topeka, Kansas, has used self-governing work teams. They determine their own hiring and firing policies, schedule their own workers, and make other major decisions that affect their work. All employees in the plant are under a single job classification, and the work teams are provided information formerly available only to management. These work teams are estimated to save Gaines $1 million a year.

Here and abroad, the semi-autonomous work groups are said to increase satisfaction and performance by (1) giving groups responsibility for selecting, training, assigning tasks, and rewarding members; (2) relying on groups to enforce productive behavior through peer pressure; (3) promoting intergroup competition; and (4) distributing resources on a group rather than individual basis.

The grand experiment in work-group design and motivation is on the drawing board at General Motors. When GM announced plans for its new car, Saturn, it also announced plans for a new way to build cars. The Saturn plant in Spring Hill, Tennessee, is to be state of the art in auto-assembly technology—a robotized, just-in-time factory—and state of the art in management and motivation as well. GM's standard seven levels of management will be reduced to five: strategic advisory committee, manufacturing advisory committee, business units, work unit modules, and the basic, organizational element—the work unit.

In July 1985, *Labor Trends* described the vision for operation of the work units at Saturn as unique: "Consensus decision making will be utilized with a strong focus on both current and near-term decisions. These units will be self-directed, integrated horizontally, and reflect synergistic group growth. These units will have responsibilities such as producing to schedule, producing a quality product, performing to budget, housekeeping, safety and health, maintenance of equipment, material and inventory control, training, job assignment, repairs, scrap control, and absenteeism. They will hold meetings, obtain supplies, keep records, seek resources as needed, and be responsible for their job preparation. They will constantly seek improvement in quality, cost, and work environment."

The reward structure to complement this work-unit focus was a central concern in the contract negotiations between GM and the United Auto Workers. The UAW agreed to give up restrictive work rules that hamper productivity and to accept guaranteed salaries—not hourly wages—of only 80 percent of the average wage paid to workers in the rest of the industry. The other 20 percent would be made up (or not) by profit-sharing and an incentive plan based on workers' performance. In exchange, GM promised lifetime job security to 80 percent of Saturn's workers and the intrinsic reward of greater participation in the workplace.

Since the announcement of the plans for Saturn, GM has drastically scaled back its plans for production and management innovation. The start-up budget has been halved, along with production and employment levels. The schedule has been slipped to at least 1992, and the company has backed away from some of its plans for plant organization. The outcome of the grand group motivation experiment at Saturn remains to be seen. A key factor will be the extent to which GM actually ties rewards to group performance.

Most companies that use team, work-group, or unit approaches to the organization rarely attach extrinsic rewards in the form of pay or bonuses to work-group performance—the group or team is simply the context within which individuals do their jobs. For example, the insurance company that prides itself on its "team concept" has no team-oriented rewards, apparently believing that being a member of a "team" is its own reward. Where rewards are tied to group performance, they are often only token acknowledgments. Perhaps this is just as well; in addition to all of the problems of measuring performance, there are significant problems with trying to manage motivation via groups. Group incentive programs typically raise touchy questions about distribution *within* the group. Did all members contribute equally? Should some group members be rewarded more than others? Should some group members be punished? Who decides who gets what? The morale-boosting, intrinsic motivational effects of being part of a group are often eroded by competing individual interests, which seem inevitably to arise in any and every group.

Group membership *is* a powerful dynamic in individual behavior; there can be no denying that. People are willing to set self-interest aside for some period of time to pursue the goals of a group or team and group norms are very powerful, but they are not always consistent with the norms of the organization. An individual's need for belonging is met just as well by his or her participation in a group of malcontents as it is by membership in a motivated group. Workers often speak with pride of how their group unity has allowed them to resist management pressure for greater productivity. Groups are quick to exert peer pressure on newcomers and "rate-busters" to keep performance within the group's norms. The stronger worker identity with the group is, the more the group manages the manager, and the less the manager manages the group.

Recent experiences with employee ownership in America shed some light on the limits of group motivators and on what it takes for group motivation to work. The dominant form of employee ownership today is the Employee Stock Ownership Plan (ESOP). There are currently over 7,000 American businesses owned wholly or in part by their workers. They are in diverse companies ranging in size from under 100 employees (e.g., Riverside Construction and Atlas Chain) to giant multinational corporations (such as ARCO and Chrysler). Close to 1,000 ESOPs, including Hallmark Cards, have majority employee ownership. More than seventy have been purchased outright. Some, like Al Tech, have received support from public agencies. Still others, like Dan River and Raymond International, have been purchased in leveraged buyouts as a response to hostile-takeover attempts. Among the ranks of employee-owned companies are some heralded successes such as Weirton Steel (employee-owned since 1981), Herman Miller, and W. L. Gore. There have also been failures—Rath Packing Company and Hyatt-Clark Industries are two recent closures.

Much of the publicity around employee ownership has focused on attempts to save jobs or prevent plant closures; however, there is also a hypothesis which suggests that employee ownership results in increased productivity. It is an extension of the group-motivation hypothesis, the idea being that employee owners care more about the company and are more motivated to work toward its success.

Peter Barnes, who for five years was president of the Solar Center in San Francisco, is convinced of it. The firm was started as a worker-owned company in 1976 and survived while hundreds of similar firms in California opened and failed. "Partly it was because we made some smart business decisions," says Barnes, "but worker ownership made a real contribution. Everyone took responsibility for the company's success. When sacrifices had to be made, we all took pay cuts and shared what work there was. The commitment came from knowing that we were in it together."

Solar Center is almost a textbook recitation of the potential motivational and productivity impact of employee ownership. But employee participation doesn't always go by the book. The Rath Packing Company was purchased by its workers in 1980. The benefits of group involvement could not overcome continuing losses and growing labor-management problems, and the company collapsed in 1983.

Hyatt-Clark Industries produced roller bearings for GM for over fifty years. In 1981 the employees bought the company after loss of a GM contract threatened to close the plant. Workers raised $53 million to buy their plant, agreed to a 25 percent pay cut, and, true to motivation theory, threw themselves into productivity and cost-cutting programs. Their motivated effort turned the company around in 1983 and 1984, and workers wanted some return on their effort—dividends and higher wages. Management demurred, even though they personally were receiving bonuses. In protest, workers staged a slowdown, in effect striking against themselves. This slowdown and foreign competition priced Hyatt-Clark out of the market, and in 1987 the company shut down.

Douglas Fraser, former president of the United Auto Workers and a member of the Hyatt-Clark board, reflected: "Hyatt-Clark was an experiment that should have worked. The problem wasn't with employee ownership, and it wasn't that the system broke down. The problem was an unwillingness to share power."[9]

Despite the promise of increased motivation via worker financial involvement, research to date suggests that employee ownership boosts motivation only where certain conditions are evident: (1) there are tangible financial rewards for employees resulting from ownership; (2) there is ongoing communication between management and workers and clear accountability; (3) there is effective planning and structure.[10] Hyatt-Clark is a case in point: an increasingly competitive market and intransigent worker-management attitudes proved to be too much for any motivational scheme to overcome. Most knowledgeable observers today believe that employee control initially increases satisfaction but, in the absence of other organizational elements, has only momentary and marginal impact upon productivity.

Management experience with group-oriented motivation schemes has highlighted the complexity of motivation in today's organizations. The manager who would be a motivator must pay attention to individuals and to groups. All the while the manager motivates individuals, he may be turning off groups and vice versa. Given these complexities, many managers have been intrigued by the notion of creating a company atmosphere that drives effort and accomplishment, motivating not just individuals or groups but entire organizations.

American managers were sensitized to the prospect that motivation may be the product of a company ethos or philosophy, more than of specific motivational processes or procedures, as a by-product of the fascination with Japanese management techniques. Terence E. Deal and Allan A. Kennedy popularized the concept of a motivating organizational ethos in their book *Corporate Cultures: The Rites and Rituals of Corporate Life.*[11] The idea of corporate culture as motivator is that individuals are most satisfied and most productive when they can identify with the mission and purposes of the organization. This important process of identification is facilitated in companies where there are clearly communicated values and belief systems, which in turn are reinforced by reward systems, rites and rituals, heroes and legends. These elements are primarily aimed at increasing individual identification with and commitment to the values of the organization, with the presumption that highly motivated performance will follow.

In some organizations the culture is so strong that the company is readily associated with it, not only in the eyes of employees but in the eyes of customers and competitors as well. For example, Hewlett-Packard is known for valuing entrepreneurship. At Digital Equipment Corporation, the emphasis is on innovation. At Delta Air Lines, the focus on customer service leads to a high value on teamwork and employees readily cross job lines to substitute in areas where they are needed. At Frito-Lay, customer satisfaction translates into a high value on quality production and service. Kodak, GE, Johnson & Johnson, and Atlantic-Richfield are other companies widely recognized as having strong cultures.

No American company better illustrates the effective use of corporate culture to motivate employees than does IBM. The shared values of IBM are clear: (1) the individual must be respected; (2) the customer must be given the best possible service; (3) excellence and superior performance must be pursued in every IBM activity. Stories of the heroic Thomas Watson are passed from one IBMer to another; the development of the PC by the Florida project team has become a company legend; trips to the training center at Armonk, New York, are rites of passage. These heroes and legends, rites and rituals all exemplify and reinforce the IBM culture, which in turn is credited with motivating the outstanding performances of IBM employees.

The loyalty and commitment of workers in companies with strong cultures is impressive, as evidenced by the testimony of employees at IBM, EDS, GE, and other excellent companies. However, a strong culture and an organizationally oriented motivation system do not necessarily lead to a motivated work force. The popular managerial perception of culture is that it is uniform, pervasive, and positive. Hence, managers and motivational consultants speak of *the* IBM culture or *the* culture at Frito-Lay. In fact, in any organization there are multiple cultures—diverse values, many rites and rituals, legends, and managerial practices—including *countercultures,* which may bind employee loyalty and commitment to behaviors that actually conflict with company goals.

One widely publicized culture/counterculture conflict has occurred at General Motors. John DeLorean was one of the first to point out that corporate and divisional cultural dictates within GM seemed to be at odds with stated company goals and philosophy. The same conflicts re-emerged in the popular business press during the much ballyhooed split between Roger Smith and EDS CEO Ross Perot in 1986 shortly after the sale of EDS to GM. These core values of GM emerge: respect authority, fit in (don't stand out or make waves), and be loyal. It is clear that the organizational atmosphere at GM motivates *conformity* over and above individual performance. The events of 1987 evidenced the lengths to which GM management would go to protect the culture—$750 million to buy out a dissenter (Perot).

While GM made headlines for its attempts to preserve its culture, Ford Motor Company has been making a major effort to *change* its culture, to move toward an organization-oriented motivation system. CEO Donald E. Peterson has said: "We don't want stars. Being part of a team is a much more productive environment." Ford, widely known under Henry Ford II for competing personalities, factionalism, and autocratic management, has recently sponsored management workshops to teach executives how to get along with one another and with their workers. The change has not come easily. Ford has eighty-two years of history to overcome at a time of tremendous economic pressure on American car makers. "Team Taurus," which developed the company's successful mid-size car line, has been a rallying point, but for every step forward there have been steps back. Of the 2,000 Ford managers given management-style tests in the company workshops, over 75 percent classified as noncreative types were comfortable with strong authority. President Harold Poling is not dismayed: "Any time you're trying to change significantly the direction of a corporate culture you have a basic level that you have to move from."[12]

That basic level Poling spoke of can run counter to motivated performance. When Willard C. Butcher of Chase Manhattan Bank wanted to redirect the financial giant, he contracted consultants to determine the company's prevailing rules of behavior. Two of the norms they discovered—"be a gentleman" and "avoid confrontations"—ran deep in the organization and worked against Butcher's new strategy. Similarly, AT&T has had difficulty changing its culture to that of a marketing company. Bell managers have had over seventy-five years of socialization into a culture that delivers service without regard to different markets or different kinds of customer cultures.

Few observers inside or outside of organizations doubt that culture plays an important role in the motivational process, but even supporters of the concept are beginning to doubt whether managers can do anything about the culture of a company, or whether it can be used to motivate employees. The director of management development for Hewlett-Packard, William P. Nilsson, has said, "I don't think [President] John Young could fundamentally change our values if he wanted to." Culture author Allan Kennedy has warned, "It costs a fortune and it takes forever." Executives estimate "forever" in this case to be between six and fifteen years.

Time, cost, and difficulty haven't yet dissuaded managers from trying to alter the culture of their companies toward organizationally oriented motivation systems, but for the most part their efforts have lacked any real coherence and fewer real results. Managers typically announce a value or belief here, initiate a ritual there, celebrate a hero somewhere else. In most companies, culture has been little more than slogans and short-lived programs. The messages to employees is a mishmash and they go on behaving pretty much as they wish. The organizational ethos is a powerful entity in employee behavior, but as a motivational plan it lacks precision. Vijay Sathe, a guru of corporate culture, concludes, "While its importance is generally accepted, culture remains an elusive and fuzzy concept."[13] Most would agree that managers need something more than elusive, fuzzy concepts to motivate employees.

A logical case can be made for a manager using any one of the three currently popular approaches to motivation. Individual pay-for-performance programs draw upon the desires of individual workers and our cultural predilection for rewarding each according to his or her contribution. Peer group pressure, the need to belong, and the sense of being part of a team drive performance in group systems. The identification with a greater purpose, i.e., the organization's mission, can spur individual efforts in a culture-focused motivation program. In theory, individual, group, and organizationally oriented systems each work, but in practice each has left something to be desired.

In most companies, managers have attempted to overcome the practical shortcomings of each of the three basic approaches to motivation by mixing motivational plans. The idea is that a hybrid system will combine the best features of each and compensate for the pitfalls of any one. The result is another mishmash. In the average company, employees are rewarded for a wide variety of behaviors—everything from showing up regularly to setting productivity records. Companies reward: *membership*—certain benefits are available by virtue of simply being employed; *tenure*—rewards often vary within companies by length of service; *attendance*—some rewards are made available to employees just as a result of their coming to work; *level/status*—many organization rewards, often including pay, change as an employee rises in the organization; *group performance*—some rewards, especially bonuses, are tied to work unit or team productivity; and *individual performance*—some rewards, but surprisingly few, are based on individual performance.

To further complicate the motivational picture in any given company, there are dozens of potential rewards to be disbursed via these six criteria. In one comprehensive listing, an IBM executive identified seventy-four separate "rewards" offered by his company, from salary to the company newsletter! Closer examination revealed that the majority of these rewards (forty) were earned simply by being an IBM employee, i.e., employment security, health benefits, ESOP, social service leave, and so on.

Attendance and tenure accounted for half of the remaining rewards, level/status another dozen. Only recognition and sales commission were earned solely as a result of individual performance. This is not unusual. Indeed, it is rare to find a company that rewards its employees solely on the basis of performance—individual or group.

What is easily overlooked in any examination of the rewards companies offer and how these are earned is how few of the rewards are indeed actually controlled by managers. All of the currently popular approaches to motivation—individual, group, and organizational—imply there is a crucial role for the manager in motivating employees. In practice, that role has proven to be mythical. Company policies and procedures regarding recognition and reward, as well as union contracts, historical precedent, and market conditions, all constrain the reward power of managers. Rarely do managers have much if any control over the elements necessary to motivate individuals, groups, or organizations. As a result of this incentive impotence, managers are not the motivators they have imagined (and expected) themselves to be, and employees know it.

In 1986 the Chicago Bears won Super Bowl XX to become the champions of professional football. Later that year, in the August preseason for the 1986–87 campaign, Bears coach Mike Ditka was critical of some of his stars for loafing. He cited Otis Wilson, Dave Duerson, and Super Bowl MVP Richard Dent for their lackluster play. Wilson responded: "We can motivate ourselves. We don't need him to motivate us. I don't have to play like it's a championship every day. I'm not going to kill myself for one man. I don't know what his problem is."

Star performers in any field, be it athletics, academics, or aerospace, are quick to point out that they don't need others to motivate them. They have their own standards of performance and they are completely capable of motivating themselves. The truth is that most employees, whatever their level of ability, feel like Wilson; however, most are not so bold as to tell their managers publicly that they are not motivators in their lives.

Presented with mixed motivational messages from their employers, most workers are of the opinion that (1) there is little linkage between individual performance and outcomes, and (2) what little linkage there is is beyond the influence of the average manager. Surveys have revealed that almost half of the work force (45 percent) believe that there is no relationship between how well they do their job and how much they are paid. Only 22 percent see a really close link between compensation and performance in their jobs. In addition, most employees do not think that they themselves will be the primary beneficiaries if they work harder and more effectively. Only 13 percent believe this. Most people believe that the benefits of increased productivity will go primarily to their employers (48 percent).[14]

Lesson number one from the myth of the motivating manager is that managers must drastically scale down their expectations of themselves as motivators. Inspirational speeches around the watercooler, slogans and productivity promotions, appeals to the higher purposes of the organization may bolster morale (or at least the manager's morale) in times of dire crises, but as day-to-day motivators these devices pale in the face of confusing and conflicting reward systems and the overriding belief on the part of employees that it doesn't matter anyway.

Once managers cast aside myths about their own role as motivators, there are some things they can do to help employees motivate themselves. A good place to begin would be with a clarification of just what managers mean by motivation. Is the measure of motivation record-breaking productivity? If so, whose productivity? Is it loyalty? How will loyalty be measured? Does high-quality production signal motivated workers? Productivity, quality, loyalty are all commonly viewed as benchmarks of a motivated work force, yet organizations and managers often reward quite different behaviors, behaviors such as attendance, tenure, position, and the like. What does it mean to be motivated?

Managers often send confusing and even conflicting messages to employees. For example, most managers gauge motivation by some calculus of effort and results. Does the employee *try* to do what is asked? Does the employee actually *accomplish* what is asked? One doesn't necessarily lead to the other. Employee efforts are often frustrated by organizational and external factors. Equipment, coworkers, the economy, and a host of other things over which he has no control may keep an employee from accomplishing what he's asked to do *in spite* of his heroic efforts. At the same time, employees can often accomplish a great deal through little or no effort on their part—the big sale that falls into the salesman's lap, the accidental breakthrough by the researcher, the manager made to look good by his people who put his presentation together. Which is likely to be more motivating, rewarding of effort without accomplishment or rewarding accomplishment without consideration of effort? Managerial accommodations can result in ambiguous motivational measures and lead to levels of effort and accomplishment on the part of workers that are measurably less than desired. Presented with a hundred drummers pounding out a hundred cadences, most workers choose to march to their own beat, saying in effect to management, "We don't need them to motivate us."

The calculus of effort and accomplishment will differ in the motivational equation from company to company, manager to manager, and from one employee to another. What remains constant, and what managers *can* affect, is employees' need for information about the specific behaviors expected of them. For all that managers cannot do to motivate employees (and there is a lot), one thing managers can do is to tell employees *what* they are expected to do and *how* they are expected to do it.

Study after study has demonstrated that a sine qua non of effort and accomplishment is that employees know what is expected of them; increasing role clarity improves task performance. Indeed, it seems as though it is not possible for managers to overcommunicate; there are no excesses where information about expectations is concerned. There are, however, some qualifiers that further elaborate the manager's role in motivation.

The first is that managers communicate both what is expected of workers and how they are expected to get there. To the extent that managers currently communicate expectations at all, they focus on the bottom line—the results to be achieved. In fact, the process, the *how* of getting there, is just as important in most companies, although it is rarely acknowledged in performance pronouncements. A major study conducted at the Center for Creative Leadership found that "specific performance problems" was only one of the ten most commonly cited reasons for managerial failure. The other nine reasons all had to do with the way work was done—insensitive to others; cold, aloof, arrogant; betrayal of trust; overly ambitious; etc.[15] The more ambiguous specific performance parameters are or the more difficult performance is to measure, the more style becomes a critical performance expectation. Everyone in the organization knows it; it's time managers admitted it.

Managers must communicate the what and the how of work behaviors and be consistent—consistent within and among what they say, what they do, and what they reward. Clarifying performance expectations is a step toward a consistent verbal message, but managers will need serious self-examination to ensure integrity between what they say they want and what they are seen to do. Perhaps the most serious malady of most of the motivation schemes managers use is that they actually undermine employee motivation. Consider, for example, the disparity between year-end bonuses to management and the coincidental Christmas bonuses to average workers. A recent Hay Group survey revealed significant differences between executive "year-end" bonuses and worker "Christmas" bonuses. In the average company, CEOs receive a year-end bonus equal to 69 percent of their annual salary; for executives the bonus is 40 percent; for managers, 21 percent. In over 75 percent of these companies, workers received no "Christmas/year-end" bonus at all; 7 percent of the companies gave hams.[16]

The year-end/Christmas bonus disparity is only one example of the status differentials that stand as disincentives to motivation in virtually every company. Daniel Yankelovich has observed

143

deep divisions in the typical American company: "Such organizations often distinguish sharply between those who manage and those who do the work—a distinction reinforced by equally sharp status differences, large pay differentials between managers and hourly workers, less constraining rules of conduct for managers, separate dining facilities, and other prerogatives that uniformly reflect the fact that managers possess power and control. Such differences also reflect the assumption that individual jobholders are less central to the success of the enterprise than are managers. Companies with this perspective see no contradiction in giving management a bonus while workers are laid off, or agree to givebacks."[17]

Some of the most compelling evidence of the effects of managerial disincentives is to be found in those American manufacturers managed by Japanese companies. In the last few years, Japanese concerns have purchased nearly 750 companies in the United States. Most of these companies were on the brink of failure under American management. General Electric gave up on a run-down, unionized special alloy plant in Michigan and sold it to Hitachi Metal in 1973. In less than two years, Hitachi Metal had it operating successfully, with the same workers and plant manager. In less than a year, Sanyo doubled employment at a bankrupt plant run by Warwick, a color-television producer. In one of the most celebrated examples, Toyota revived a unionized auto plant in California that had been virtually abandoned by General Motors. Toyota pledged that management would cut its own salaries first before rank-and-file employees would be asked to accept temporary concessions during economic downturns.

Yoshi Tsurumi, president of the Pacific Basin Center Foundation, attributes the success of Japanese operators in America to the absence of disincentives from management: "American executives too often act as a privileged class, asking sacrifices of workers that they have no intention of making themselves. While they preach democracy and the need to work together, they dictate work rules and vote themselves raises while workers are laid off. This behavior, not the rhetoric, is what American workers perceive as their bosses' true beliefs. It is this behavior that employees respond to with absenteeism, shoddy workmanship, and drug abuse."[18]

Not all American firms flaunt managerial disdain for the common worker with such actions as the juxtaposition of worker layoffs and executive bonuses. However, in every company there are small points of difference between the value of management and the value of workers that add up to major motivational disincentives. Reserved parking spaces and health club memberships are not invisible to employees. They may not seem like a big deal unless you are a worker who doesn't have them and the manager asking you to work harder and accomplish more does. Reducing the disincentives by eliminating arbitrary status differentials large and small (big bonuses and free coffee) may be the most difficult thing for managers to do because it requires self-examination and personal sacrifice. Once managers have made it clear that they intend to support their words with their actions, the deck is cleared for proving it to workers by rewarding the behaviors management seeks.

Employees must also experience a consistent relationship between doing what is asked of them and receiving the rewards they desire. Managers must make every effort to identify accurately outstanding performers and reward them accordingly. It is true that the rewards do not have to be monetary. Years of research have established the reward value of recognition, participation, autonomy, and other responses to the needs of employees. In the process, managers (at the urging of academics) have underemphasized—even overlooked—the importance of *pay* as a motivator. Intrinsic motivators notwithstanding, pay remains the primary criterion by which jobs are valued by everyone—workers and managers alike. Employees use pay as the measure of their value to the company, their relative value vis-à-vis other employees, and as a yardstick of personal success. Beyond its fundamental importance to employees, money takes on added value as a motivator because it is the single most flexible reward a company has to offer. Employees may use it in any way they see fit, to fulfill whatever needs they have. Unlike promotions and favored assignments, monetary rewards in the form of pay, bonuses, and stock options can easily be adjusted up or down, and they can be applied continuously; they do not "top out." Given its universal applicability and inherent flexibility, it may be that there is no single motivator more powerful than money. Managers would be well advised to remember that.

Unfortunately, most companies severely restrict the extent to which managers can use money to reward performance of their employees. Most companies take pay-for-performance decisions completely out of the hands of managers, further diminishing managers' scant opportunities to motivate employees. Forced performance rankings (i.e., "No more than 10 percent of your employees may be in the highest ranking") and rigorous adherence to salary schedules remove managers' discretionary use of monetary rewards and eliminate a potentially powerful tool to motivate employees. Many managers are just as happy to be relieved of the responsibility for managing salaries and bonuses. They are uncomfortable with the ambiguities of assessing performance and, to some extent, are embarrassed by their limited powers to reward performance when and where it does appear. It is in many respects easier simply to have the entire process taken out of their hands, and they are reluctant to push for greater discretionary power over pay and performance.

For every manager who doesn't desire more control over the motivational process, there are hundreds who believe that they not only have control over the necessary elements of motivation, but that they *are* the motivators. It is a myth encouraged by modern management thinking; paradoxically, it is a myth encouraged by the complexity of motivation. The motivation equation today involves *management practices*—individual reward practices, group and unit rewards, organization culture; *job characteristics*—autonomy, variety, feedback, intrinsic rewards; and the *characteristics of individual jobholders and managers*—attitudes toward self, toward the job, toward the organization's needs, and much more.

In the face of this complexity, it is seductive to think that someone is responsible and that there are simple things to be done. In fact, there are only a few things that managers can do and those things can only create the conditions for workers to motivate themselves; they cannot motivate workers. This has been interpreted by some as a strong case for companies hiring "self-starters" and "high achievers"—meaning, to many, MBAs. MBAs may be as much of a myth as the motivating manager.

7

The Myth of the MBA

It's hard to convince myself that the world needs
70,000 or so MBAs a year.
> —*Robert K. Jaedicke,*
> *Dean, Stanford Business School*

These kids are smart. But I'd as soon take a python
to bed as hire one. He'd suck my brains, memorize
my Rolodex, and use my telephone to find some
other guy who'd pay him twice the money.
> —*Ned Dewey,*
> *Harvard MBA, '49*

In 1960, the nation's three dozen graduate business schools
granted 4,643 Master of Business Administration degrees. Currently, over 650 schools churn out in excess of 70,000 MBAs a
year and companies of every size are snapping them up at salaries
well over $35,000. The growth of the MBA degree over the last
twenty-five years has been truly staggering—a twenty-fold increase in the number of degree-granting institutions and graduates. What is more, there is no sign of slackening in the popularity
of the degree; at present, over 200,000 students are training to
become "the future business leaders of America." Dean Robert
K. Jaedicke of the Stanford Business School observes, "If you look
at the growth rate over the past twenty-five years, you could
come to the conclusion that everybody in the U.S. will have an
MBA degree by the year 2010."

The question is, "When (if) everyone in America has an MBA,
will American business be better off?" Cynics suggest that the
last thing American business needs is even one more MBA! They
point to the downhill course of major economic events and in-

dicators during the twenty-five years of runaway MBAs. Even in the face of the most pro-business administration since Calvin Coolidge, the American economy has remained troubled. The deficit is at an all-time high, suffering from adverse trade balances in consumer goods, high technology, even food. All of this against competitors from Japan, Korea, South America, Canada, France, West Germany—countries without the "benefits" of a managerial class with MBAs. Gains in productivity have been disappointingly small. Large numbers of blue-collar workers and middle managers have lost jobs; those that still have jobs have frequently been compelled to accept wage or salary cuts. Unemployment sticks at 7 percent, a figure that as recently as the 1960s spelled economic and political crisis. Imagine what dire straits the economy would be in without MBAs.

Of course, correlation is not causation. The mere fact that the rise of MBAs in this country coincides with the decline of the economy does not lead to the conclusion that one causes the other. The proliferation of MBAs is not the cause of the poor performance of the economy, but the persistent belief in the value of the MBA has certainly contributed to what is wrong with American management. The myth of the MBA distorts the way problems are perceived and actions are conceived. This distortion is pervasive; it affects employers, would-be graduates, and business educators, each of whom buys into and bolsters the myth of the MBA and furthers the damaging, even debilitating, distortions.

In 1985, the average starting salary for a Harvard MBA was $44,500. MBA holders from Dartmouth, MIT, Wharton, Stanford, Virginia, and Yale were all greeted by starting salaries in excess of $40,000. Starting salaries at the remaining dozen of the top twenty business schools averaged in the high thirties. And these are only *averages*. The top schools reported highest offers of $80,000 and up for their MBA graduates. The booty for business grads doesn't stop with starting salaries in the high five figures; signing bonuses, clothing allowances, and payoffs of student loans are all standard elements in the recruiting packages companies use to lure the best and the brightest from B-schools. It's no wonder that students are applying for admission to MBA programs in record numbers. Even tuition costs in excess of $20,000 for the two-year curriculum at the best schools have not dissuaded applicants; the better schools continue to enjoy record applicant pools. Most would-be future business leaders look upon it as an investment. As one MBA student observes, "I'm in hock up to my ears but by this time next year, I expect to sign on with a company who will erase my debt and pay me $80,000 a year. Two years of poverty to start at eighty plus sounds like a pretty good deal to me."

Corporate America has contributed to the myth of the MBA by creating a seller's market for the degree. The high entry salaries companies are willing to pay for MBAs are the most often noted feature of this market. However, even if salaries were to drop to more reasonable levels, the market would continue to be strong because companies have made the MBA a condition of employment and/or promotion. The MBA has become a prerequisite to get in the door, and, once in, to move up the ladder. In the majority of the *Fortune* 500 companies, entry into the ranks of management is possible only upon completion of an MBA program (and usually a top-level program at that). Some companies go so far as to limit their recruiting/hiring to certain schools. The consulting firm McKinsey & Company hires almost exclusively from the Harvard and Stanford MBA programs. For many years, the Trammell Crow real estate development company would interview only at Harvard. Goldman Sachs has long had a penchant for Wharton grads. The message is getting through about the halo effect companies attribute to certain MBA programs. A student in Chicago's MBA program comments, "By going to an elite business school I'm giving a signal of my potential for success." The elite schools can afford to be super selective. Yale accepts 20 percent of its applicants, Harvard 18 percent, Stanford 9 percent. Many MBA students at "lesser" schools learn too late that to be eligible for the best jobs and the biggest money, just having an MBA is not enough. The remaining 630-plus schools that offer the MBA program feed off the allure that companies have bestowed on the degree and off the applicant castoffs from the best schools. "Many of these schools come very close to selling the degree," say Raymond E. Miles, dean of the University of California–Berkeley B-school. Harvard's Dean John McArthur maintains that 97 percent of the schools that offer the degree admit "virtually anyone who applies."

In many respects, corporate insistence on the MBA at the entry level is a way of limiting the applicant pool rather than a performance-based job requirement. A *Business Week* survey of 600 senior executives revealed that the majority felt an MBA had little to do with job performance and made little difference in employee merit or ability. However, these same executives admitted that their company interviewed *only* MBAs for their management-trainee positions. Perhaps most revealing, when asked, "If your son or daughter were planning a career in business, would you advise him or her to get an MBA?," 78 percent of executives would advise the MBA.

Walter Wriston, chairman of New York's Citibank, who has no MBA, has said: "We look on the MBA degree as a tough filter through which people pass. It's one that lets them hit the deck running. But after you've been around a few months, nobody asks you where you went to school. They ask: 'What can you do?'" Other executives agree. Says Samuel Armacost, a Stanford MBA who took over as president of the Bank of America: "There's nothing magical about the MBA. It's just natural selection. If you hire the top 10 percent from the top three or four business schools, your expectations will generally be met in the course of time."

Luther Hodges, Jr., a Harvard MBA who was chairman of the National Bank of Washington, sees the MBA as a seasoning experience: "I tend to think we look for MBAs, but to me it is not so much the business expertise as it is the additional education or maturing. We do not like to hire somebody just out of college. Age twenty-one, that's too young. Graduate school after military service, age twenty-five or twenty-six, that's even better.

Graduate school plus the military and some work, that's better still. Not because of how much talent they bring, but they are settled down. They were knocked around a little bit."[1]

A key human resource executive offers this candid appraisal of the MBA in his telecommunications company: "Look, it's become a union card pure and simple. The most the MBA says about anyone is that they've been able to survive another two years of school. We know it doesn't tell us any more than that about what they can or can't do, it doesn't matter, we'll teach them how to do it our way anyway. When it comes right down to it, we require an MBA for two reasons. One, it means just that many fewer people that we need to interview. And, two, we have so many MBAs around here now if we brought someone in who didn't have one, they'd probably croak from insecurity."

These observations suggest why corporate America is where it is regarding MBAs and why it's getting worse. There are some colorful analogies about the proliferation of MBAs in business. One such line compares MBAs to coat hangers: "Put two of them in a room, close the door, and in the morning you'll have two dozen." Another approach likens MBAs to peanuts or potato chips: "You can't have just one." There is a kernel of truth in both of these analogies. MBAs do seem to spawn MBAs, and there is a logic to this.

Quantitative management methods introduced to business in the 1950s (PERT/CPM) carried with them the seeds of the MBA myth that has culminated in today's bumper crop of MBAs. The quantitative methods required analytical skills most managers of the 1950s and 1960s, trained as they were in the school of hard knocks, did not have. Corporations turned to universities for state-of-the-art skills and brought economists, financial analysts, and market analysts into headquarters: thus began the march of the MBAs. A broadcast executive describes the march through his company:

The president brought an MBA on board as his financial analyst. No sooner was he at work than he started demanding a lot of data that we didn't have. He wanted this report from accounting, these numbers from marketing, audits from personnel, and so on. We had to hire a second MBA to put together a management information system to provide the data the first MBA asked for. The system he designed was so complex that the Accounting Department and the Marketing Department had to hire MBAs to understand and feed the system. From there on I honestly don't know how much of it was driven by need and how much was driven by status, but it seemed like everybody just had to have an MBA on their staff. And not just at corporate; the operating units starting hiring MBAs, too. In the space of about three or four years, we went from having *no* MBAs to hiring *only* MBAs. Now we're in phase two of the MBA mania; all of our old managers who don't have MBAs want to go back and get one![2]

It happened and continues to happen in most companies just as it happened for this broadcaster. One MBA analyst creates the need for another analyst and another MBA. Nearly one-half of the MBAs graduating in the eighties went into consulting and staff jobs. Managers without the MBA see these high-paid fast-trackers and become both envious and insecure; they see money and opportunity passing them by. How to catch up? Get back to school and get an MBA. It's a perception reinforced by employers. More than one middle manager has been told that in order to be promoted he or she is going to have to "broaden" or "update skills." The surest evidence of self-development for plateaued lower- and middle-level managers is the MBA and, what's more, the company will pay the tuition.

"I was flat out told by my boss that without the MBA he wouldn't be able to convince *his* boss that I was worthy of promotion. I can see his point; at the next level up I'd be managing people who have MBAs. It could be awkward if I didn't have mine." Many managers do seek the MBA because they feel pressure from their company to come "up to speed" with one. As more MBAs are hired, the pressure to have an MBA in order to manage MBAs (whether or not there is merit in this argument) increases. Companies have also relied heavily upon the MBA to broaden managers, especially as preparation for moving them from a functional specialization, such as engineering or accounting, to more generalist duties. A Texas Instrument executive comments: "We've basically used the area universities as trainers charged with making managers out of our engineers. Our tuition-reimbursement bill is astronomical because, of course, you can't encourage a few to go back and get the MBA very long before everyone else figures out that that is the approved path. We have so many people going for MBAs that we hold some classes in the plants instead of on campus."[3]

TI is not alone in its encouragement and use of MBA programs for employees. Companies with large concentrations of employees in certain locales dominate enrollments in area MBA programs. In recent years, the most dramatic growth in MBA enrollments has been in the evening, part-time, and executive MBA programs that cater to older, more experienced, working students. Degree-granting institutions, aware of the declining population in the eighteen to twenty-four age group over the next fifteen years, have been very creative in responding to the needs of the working MBA candidate. Part-time programs offer evening classes, at some schools every night of the week. The diligent student can complete the degree in three to five years. Some MBA programs offer opportunities for the part-time student to speed up his or her matriculation with intensive classroom experiences, i.e., a six-day course which meets eight hours a day for six consecutive days. The academic credibility of the course is ostensibly maintained because contact hours (i.e., hours in the classroom between student and professors) are equal to those of traditional semester courses. The intensive scheduling appeals to students in part-time programs because they can use vacation time to go to school and speed up their degree.

The real growth segment of the MBA industry appears to be the executive MBA program. Part-time programs cater to stu-

dents five to ten years out of school looking to prepare themselves for promotion or for career changes. Executive MBA
programs are designed for senior managers with significant
managerial experience and responsibility. These are high-ticket,
high-profile programs that advertise star-quality faculty, distinguished guest speakers, personal computers, and international
education tours. The participants are often motivated by the
same desires to get ahead, catch up, cross over, but more often
than not, executive MBAs are looking to be retooled and regen-
erated. As the division manager of an aerospace firm commented: "I've been managing for over twenty years and I saw
myself in a rut, handling the same problems in the same way
day after day. The executive MBA was a chance for me to
change my company, my job, and myself in a new way. The
degree is not important to me. At my age I don't need the
credential; I'm in it for the learning."

Whatever the motivation of the executive MBA student, the
message sent by the boss going back to school is received far
down the line. Pressured from above by the boss's example and
from below by new hires bearing MBAs, everyone in between
seems to be clamoring to get an MBA. Company tuition-reimbursement plans are an added inducement, and formal and informal promotional policies an additional incentive. Corporate
America says you have to have an MBA to get in, and you have
to have an MBA to get further up; these messages go a long way
toward promoting the myth of the MBA.

Corporate America supports the myth of the MBA in yet another way: companies make no effort to change MBA programs.

With all corporate America does to promote the MBA, it is
clear that corporations can and do have a great deal of influence
over what transpires in the programs. This influence is all the
greater when one realizes the financial support business schools
receive from the corporate community. Corporate gifts account
for the overwhelming majority of nontuition dollars available to
a business school—money to endow facilities and faculties, money
for scholarships, money for research. Some corporate gifts are
given with such regularity that they are built into the operating

budgets of the recipient schools. Major business schools can and do count on annual contributions from the Big Eight accounting firms, the major banks and investment houses, and the large firms headquartered in their locale or simply those firms who want first shot at recruiting students from the best schools. In a very real sense, companies *pay* business schools to provide an MBA for their prospective employees and, through tuition reimbursements, for their current employees. Corporations *could* exercise powerful influence over MBA programs, but they don't. By their negligence, corporations further the myth of the MBA.

Surveys throughout the eighties by Arthur Young & Company (1981) and Louis Harris & Associates Inc. (1986) show executives split on whether the contribution of employees with MBAs is superior to those without MBAs. There is overwhelming agreement that, relative to their contributions, the starting salaries for MBAs are too high. Experienced executives are similarly unanimous in their views that MBAs are high on quantitative methods and high on theory, but low in understanding how it should be applied in practice, that they are technique-bound with little comprehension of real industrial problems, and that they lack the necessary personal skills to become effective managers. In addition, MBAs are generally perceived by executives to be impatient and to have unrealistic expectations about how fast they should progress in their careers.

Executives have been very outspoken in their criticisms of MBAs and MBA programs. Said Thomas B. Hubbard, founder and chairman of THinc., a New York consulting firm: "They tend to be more loyal to their personal careers than to any company. So although they have made some companies better, they have also made them more vulnerable." "They are often inexperienced, arrogant, highly individualistic operators with no patience for team effort," said Nelson Cornelius, manager of Merrill Lynch. James Bere, an Northwestern MBA and chairman of Borg-Warner, commented: "We are slowing the pace in recruiting MBAs. They can be too bottom-line oriented, looking inward rather than outward. MBAs are often quite impatient, and they can be a bit condescending toward others. They forget it takes time and patience to learn customers and their needs."[4]

Stanley Marcus, former chairman of Neiman-Marcus, faults MBAs for their lack of humor, their lack of humility, and their lack of humanity: "Although the MBAs generally see themselves as the best and the brightest, the most energetic and ambitious, a growing number of corporate managers look on them as arrogant amateurs, trained only in figures and lacking experience in both the manufacture of goods and the handling of people. In the pantheon of young business executives, there are gods of success, diligence, alertness, punctuality, timing, and memo writing. But, alas, there is none for humor, which I view with dismay."

Chief executive officers surveyed by Cornell University feel that MBAs need more attention to human values in the workplace.[5] Comments from the surveyed presidents included "MBAs are not team players," and "MBAs have too little people sensitivity. Many seem to believe that good analytical skills coupled with knowledge of computers is sufficient. It is not."

Owners and operators of small businesses are even more critical of MBAs than are their megafirm counterparts. Barry Wells, owner of an east Texas printing and office supply concern, says, "Of course we can't afford to hire MBAs in the first place, but even if we could I doubt that we would. From what I've seen and heard of them, they would cause more problems than they would solve. In a small business you have to be willing to do everything with everybody; you can't afford to have anyone who considers themselves to be above certain jobs or above certain people. I'm sure there are some nice-guy MBAs who might fit right in but no MBA program prepares them for small business. MBAs are for big companies and big companies are for MBAs— some might say they deserve each other."[6]

In fact, in their structure and style, small businesses do not lend themselves to a proliferation of MBAs. Certainly the salary demands and interpersonal skills of MBAs do not lend themselves to small-business careers. One MBA graduate who found himself taking a small-business job (admittedly out of desperation) gave this advice: "There are some things I learned in the MBA program that have been useful but, frankly, most of the courses were geared toward jobs with the giants. Around here I've found it works better if I don't even tell people that I have an MBA. If they knew, they'd only hold it against me."

Overly analytical and underhumanized, overpaid and underskilled, impatient and insensitive, these are not the only criticisms of MBAs that executive of firms large and small express strongly. Significant numbers of business leaders are critical of MBAs' written and oral presentation skills, their awareness of social and political events, their knowledge of sales and manufacturing (as opposed to marketing and strategy), their exposure to international business, and their business ethics. It is reasonable to assume that in the face of these many corporate criticisms of MBAs and MBA programs and, with the considerable resources at their disposal (tuition supports, scholarships, gifts), corporate leaders would use their considerable clout to change MBA programs and thereby change the product they purchase. It is a reasonable assumption but it is erroneous.

Despite being on record as having serious concerns about MBA programs and their products, on the financial side—where it counts—corporate America is in strong support of MBA programs and their products as they exist, warts and all. Jerry Harvey, professor of management science at George Washington University, notes, "Business education reflects exactly what people in the business world want. We've designed organizations that reward people who think very narrowly and behave very narrowly." According to Harvey and others, corporations, whatever their criticisms of MBA programs, are getting *exactly* what they are paying for. The dean of Dartmouth's Tuck School makes the case pointedly: "I don't pay our graduates $35,000 a year; Wall Street does. I can keep them reasonably humble when I grade their papers, but when Wall Street tells them they are God's gift to investment banking, then I have a real problem. They begin to believe it."

What corporate America *says* it wants and what it will pay

for are two different things when it comes to MBAs. Ironically, companies are willing to pay top dollar for a product that is far less than they say they want. A senior vice-president of the First Atlanta Corporation has said, "If I could choose one degree for the people I hire, it would be English. I want people who can read and speak in the language we're dealing with. You can teach a group of Cub Scouts to do portfolio analysis." Ask *that* executive how much money his company has contributed to the English Department at Emory or Georgia Tech. Has it established scholarships for undergraduates with English degrees who want to pursue an MBA? Has it endowed a chair in business communications? The answer to each of these questions is no, and this Georgia company is not alone. A partner at the accounting firm of Ernst & Whinney has complained, "We get a lot of bright young accountants but they can't make it as managers. They can't seem to handle the people side of the business whether it's outside with clients or inside managing their own people." This partner chairs the local office's corporate gift committee, which makes a major contribution to the area business school each year—not to the Organization Behavior Department or to the Marketing Department, where students might learn about relating to colleagues and to clients, but instead to the Accounting Department, where students learn more about crunching numbers.

Where the opinions of corporate executives about MBAs and MBA programs really count is not in surveys and polls but in scholarships, professorships, and support grants. In 1959, two major reviews of business education, one by the Ford Foundation and one by the Carnegie Corporation, criticized business schools for their lack of academic rigor. At that time, the corporate community made a commitment to underwrite the move toward more analytical education for business. Corporate gifts to business schools have increased every year for the last twenty-five years. Today, along with the increased giving, there is increased criticism from the same supporting corporate community that business schools have become too quantitative and theoretical. Graduate business schools must have a clear mandate for change if they are to revitalize and humanize their curricula. Such a mandate is emerging as the responses of chief executives demonstrate. But the message is not yet forceful enough to have a meaningful impact on how the next generation of managers is trained because the message to change conflicts with the message to stay the same implied by financial support of the status quo. To date, corporate America has not changed its support of MBA programs to reflect its avowed changed views of the MBA. Until such monetary mandates are present, corporate America can only be seen as contributing further to the myth that the MBA is what it presumes to be, "preparation of America's future business leaders." Certainly prospective students see no change in the value of the MBA, and their participation in the myth is as important to its promulgation as is the participation of the business community and the business schools.

It is difficult to fault students for this. As one potential investment banker confided, "If I had my druthers, I'd druther be in English lit., but, hell, there just aren't a lot of people out there willing to pay $40,000 for an English lit. major. The way I figure it, I may not love my work as an investment banker but at least I'll be able to afford to buy all the books I want to read." One might decry the instrumental outlook and materialistic values of today's MBAs or denounce their conservatism and their narrowness, but they cannot be denied their right to make a living. It's like pushing a rock uphill to convince them that they might be happier and even more successful by pursuing some route other than the MBA. In fact, the aims of would-be MBAs are no different from that of their prospective employers. They want to be business leaders and they are eager to learn whatever will help them to achieve that end. They expect that an MBA will be their admission ticket into the privileged managerial class. The widely publicized successes of their predecessors—the six-figure salaries and vice-presidencies achieved seemingly upon graduation—fuel their expectations of rapid promotion and prosperity. While we can hope that students might aspire to some higher goal than holding a Platinum American Express card, it is hard to criticize them for taking advantage of the bounteous opportunity the MBA affords. When examined closely, it is not opportunism that marks MBA students; it is their gullibility. One student has described it as "the MBA make-over."

"It's a lot like the make-overs in the glamour magazines. You know, the ones where they show this really blah picture of someone who looks like they're on the verge of death, then, two pages later with makeup, a new hairdo, new wardrobe and accessories, she's made into a beauty queen. Getting an MBA is a lot like that. Most of my classmates were like me, sitting in some do-nothing–go-nowhere job. Then you see an article or a school brochure and you read about somebody your age who got an MBA and now has an exciting job and a megabuck salary and you say, 'Hey, I could do that!' So, you look around, find a school that will take you, and it's 'Look out world, here I come.' The MBA-made-over, new, successful me."

Students would be well advised to be a little bit more cynical about the value of an MBA. As degree-granting institutions and degree-holders proliferate, the market value of the degree diminishes. John P. Evans, former president of the American Assembly of Collegiate Schools of Business (AACSB), the accrediting agency of business schools, observes, "I do have the sense that corporations, particularly at the MBA level, are getting more selective in their recruiting activities—many of them are going to fewer schools; they're taking a more focused approach to their hiring." Professor Evans has captured what is happening to the MBA phenomenon. With 70,000 MBAs graduating annually, the 10 percent graduating from the top twenty schools will find themselves much in demand, but graduates from the "lesser" schools may find that they are no more marketable than they were prior to the MBA. They're not wined and dined by recruiters from the *Fortune* 500, and they're not offered signing bonuses and salaries in the high forties. Indeed, they may discover that they would have been better off to invest two additional years in their career instead of two years in getting a run-of-the-mill MBA.

Ernie Stanton graduated as an agricultural economics major

from a solid midwestern university. Upon graduation he went to work for a large midwestern agribusiness concern as a trainee purchasing agent. Diffident but bright, Ernie saw more aggressive MBA graduates hired into the firm at salaries almost double his and at jobs with much greater potential for advancement. He decided the MBA would make him into the executive type he envied. Too late to apply to the really top schools, Ernie applied to a mid-level MBA program. Once there, he did well in the classroom and used his out-of-class time to acquaint himself with, and acquire, the mindset of his fellow students. Like 80 percent of his peers, he aspired to a job in investment banking or with a venture capital firm, but no such offers were forthcoming. The top firms didn't even recruit at Ernie's school. One and one-half years after graduation, Ernie had still not found a job he wanted and he was forced to take a job with a telephone collection agency.

What went wrong? For one, the MBA make-over did not take. In the classroom, Ernie did fine (3.5 on a 4.0 scale) but nothing in the MBA program addressed Ernie's *real* learning needs. One professor wrote: "Ernie does not present himself well. He still comes across as being too shy. He has a weak handshake and doesn't look you in the eye when you meet him. Although he is always clean, his physical appearance is poor. He does not know how to dress well, even with his casual clothes. The only way he will get a job is if someone is willing to take a real risk because the first impression is terrible." In retrospect, Dale Carnegie might have done more for Ernie than an MBA program; at least it wouldn't have led to galloping career expectations.

As Ernie now reflects, "From the moment you first read the marketing brochure to the moment you hear the graduation speech, you're bombarded with success stories. There's all this reinforcing going on that says you've made the right choice, you'll get a great job, you'll be offered a huge salary. Look at all the people just like you who came here for their MBA and have gone on to make it big. Even if you didn't want to believe it you'd end up believing it, and most of us wanted to believe it in the first place so we bought it in a big way. Later you find out your school isn't good enough to attract the really top companies and the few really good jobs go to people with lots of prior experience who left good jobs to get an MBA. I would have been much better off to stay where I was. All the MBA did was to raise my expectations."

The gullibility of students, the belief that the MBA represents their best chance to make it big, is matched by the promotional materials of the business schools. The result is rising expectations and, ultimately, rampant underemployment. Ernie is not alone. There is a glut of MBAs, especially in the currently in-vogue fields such as finance and banking. Large numbers of MBAs end up working at jobs for which they feel their training has made them both overqualified and underpaid. Recession and the resulting downsizing in many industries have hit particularly hard at MBA-level positions, which further exacerbates the problem of underemployed MBAs. A young MBA from a reputable midwestern school is a night security guard, a woman with an MBA in international management and fluent in three languages is a saleswoman in an upscale boutique. A geophysicist who left his position in the declining oil industry to retool with an MBA has taken a job cleaning computer discs for a mortgage banker; he hopes he'll be able to move laterally within the company once he's in the door. The stories of similar dreams deferred describe the countless MBA graduates who are not featured in the B-school brochures.

It is difficult to assess exactly how many MBAs end up underemployed, but recent studies have suggested that as many as 40 percent of U.S. workers believe they have skills that they are unable to use in their jobs. The figures for MBAs are undoubtedly higher. No one, especially not prospective students, seems to ask, "If there are 70,000 MBAs awarded this year, are there 70,000 jobs available that *require* an MBA?" On a smaller scale, the 185 incoming members of the MBA class at a major regional business school were asked, "How many of you intend to concentrate in finance?" One hundred and sixty-five students raised their hands.

When informed that out of the previous class fewer than 10 percent had found jobs as financial analysts, they were undaunted. The impression was that no data, anecdotal or empirical, would sway their thinking. They were full of expectations of the program and of themselves. And they were sure to be disappointed.

Positive thinking is a powerful force and there is no absence of it among MBAs, but they would do well to moderate their expectations of themselves and their degree with a dose of reality and probability. One wishes that MBA students would bring to the decision to get an MBA, or what field to get an MBA in, some of the same analytical rigor that they apply to their subsequent studies. This rigor is not going to come from companies that long ago decided to focus only on the outstanding MBAs from the outstanding programs. These companies don't care if there is any value to an MBA for a marginal student in a marginal program. Reality testing will certainly not come from the business schools, which, for reasons of survival, must present themselves as holders of the keys to the kingdom. Reality testing must come from students acting as involved, informed consumers asking, "What value will I receive for my money?" "How else might I spend the next two years?" "Is it worth it?" As long as students eschew this reflection and introspection in favor of the MBA make-over, they will continue to play right into the hands of the business schools, the **third** partner in purveying the myth of the MBA.

A New York financial consultant, a former partner with Lehman Brothers, the investment banking firm, has seen the brightest MBAs from the best of schools. His observation: "A lot of what is preached at business schools today is absolute rot. It is paper management. It is not the management of hard resources and people. Business schools teach that business is nothing but numbers—and the numbers only for the next quarter." "Absolute rot" may be an extreme characterization, but there are a lot of people in and out of business and business schools who have some serious reservations about what goes on in MBA programs. Ask any CEO his or her opinion of business school offerings and you unleash a litany of curricular shortcomings that runs the gamut from business ethics to business etiquette, from how to decide to how to dress. The criticisms are particularly biting when the economy is under pressure and everyone is searching for a scapegoat. Business schools are particularly easy targets.

Setting aside executive frustration, intra-university jealousy, and squabbles among competing programs, there are some grounds for questioning MBA curricula in five specific areas: (1) MBA programs overemphasize quantitative analysis and financial maneuvering; (2) with this overemphasis, there is a corresponding "dehumanization" of management; (3) MBA programs present an oversimplified perspective on management, which is characterized by the case approach, the CEO view, and the absence of interdisciplinary work; (4) there is inadequate attention to learning the business—especially production and manufacturing; (5) there is little attention to international business.

The most common first jobs of MBAs from the top schools are in finance, banking, and consulting. It is either cause or consequence (or both) that the core curricula/required courses in the top schools are dominated by finance, accounting, and quantitative methods. A quick trip to representative schools from coast to coast reveals that the prospective business leaders of America are hard at work "crunching numbers." At the prestigious Stanford Graduate School of Business, the first year of coursework prescribes Accounting I and II, Decision Making, Decision Support Models, Economic Analysis, Analysis of Productive Systems, Data Analysis, Business Finance, Marketing Management, and Organization Behavior. The University of Chicago is generally regarded as the most theoretical of the MBA programs with required courses such as Applied Econometrics and Application of Financial Theory. But at its esteemed neighbor, the Kellogg School of Northwestern, things are scarcely better. There the required courses for an MBA student are Accounting for Decision Making, Mathematical Methods for Management Decisions, Statistical Methods for Management Decision, Microeconomic Analysis, Finance, Operations Management, Computer Workshop,

Marketing, Managing of Organizations, and Organization Behavior. At the Fuqua School of Business at Duke, the pattern of required courses heavy on quantitative analysis is repeated: Managerial Economics, Economic Environment of the Firm, Managerial Accounting, Financial Accounting, Financial Management, Statistical Analysis, Quantitative Analysis, Operations Management, Computers, Marketing Management, Organization Behavior, and Business Communications.

The required coursework is no more balanced at the lesser schools, which, after all, take their lead from the top programs. Even at "Obscure University," prospective MBAs are put through the numbers, by the numbers. Defenders of the status quo argue the MBA programs are so laden with quantitative analysis because they are responding to the marketplace, giving businesses and students the product they want. One dean comments, "I would say our curriculum, put to the market test, is well designed. We have no problem attracting students and no problem placing students. The quantitative skills orientation seems to satisfy employers, students, and, just as importantly, faculty. Until there is some measurable dissatisfaction from one of these groups, I don't see the need to change."

"Measurable dissatisfaction" is unlikely to come from business school faculty. The growth of business school enrollments and faculty has put many business schools on the defensive within their own universities. Other university disciplines complain that business schools draw high-quality students away from their graduate programs and that the burgeoning business school faculties monopolize scarce university resources, such as research funds, salaries, and tenure appointments. As a defense, business schools have pushed their faculties for more academic rigor—meaning more research publications. This finds favor with many new business school professors who have little or no business experience and are more comfortable with the models and theories that are the stuff of academic publishing. The result is deeper and more complex analysis of narrower and narrower problems. This line of inquiry is reflected in MBA coursework.

Business school faculty see no reason to alter the quantitative emphasis of the MBA curriculum; it serves their professional needs and they believe that it serves the needs of students. "Besides," as one faculty member notes, "we only dictate one-half of their schedule. They have plenty of electives that they can use for the soft courses they want to take." Most programs do offer MBAs some measure of choice, especially in their second year. Of course, most MBA students use their elective choices to take more courses in financial analysis. This is what many students intended to do all along. Over one-half of entering MBA students *intend* to go into finance, banking, or consulting (read: economic analysis). By the end of the first year, the number approaches 80 to 85 percent as students have been effectively socialized by their required coursework to see that "quant jocks" are the stars of any MBA class; they are the ones that get the best offers from business.

And so it comes back to business. Are MBA programs so heavily quantitative because business wants MBAs who are "quant jocks"? What of all the business community criticism of organizationally naïve number crunchers? The vice-president of a restaurant chain captures the sentiment of many executives: "The business schools seem to have forgotten the age-old definition of management—getting things done through *people*, not through analyses, not through probabilistic statistics, not through econometrics. Through people. The trick today is to find an MBA that knows anything about people, someone who hasn't had all the humanity crunched out of them by the numbers."

Though business has its concerns and criticisms about MBAs and MBA programs, to date their actions do not support their words. Competition among firms for the top "quant jocks" from the top MBA schools seems to grow more fierce with each new graduating class. But there is a glimmer of evidence that someone may be listening to what business executives are saying. Some schools are beginning to respond to critics of MBA programs that produce "narrow-minded technicians who lack interpersonal and communication skills." At Yale, Dean Burton G. Malkiel says,

"We want our people well trained in quantitative methods. But the most important thing people can know is how to get along with and motivate others." At Carnegie-Mellon, several "soft" courses have been introduced: Crisis Management, taught by former American Motors Corporation chairman Gerald C. Meyers, is one; The Gold-Collar Worker, a class that advises students on how best to motivate the growing ranks of "knowledge workers" in service businesses, is another.

"Soft" course additions to MBA curricula will have to expand dramatically if there is to be any hope of striking a balance with required quantitative courses. Even with the current course additions, any change in the MBA product is likely to be a long time in coming—soft courses are added only as elective choices, not as substitutes for required "crunchers." Moreover, given the manner in which MBAs are educated, it may be that no amount of soft coursework will produce "humanized" MBAs.

It is the nearly consensual view of executives that MBAs are lacking in humility, humor, and humanity—all valued skills for executives. A poll of 480 chief executive officers asked, "Have you found that younger executives with MBA degrees have a greater or lesser sense of humor than others?" The vast majority of those responding checked "Lesser." The need for a sense of humor is not unknown to business schools, only ignored. Most of the 170 business school deans who were queried in the same poll acknowledged that there was probably a correlation between humor and executive success, but they generally agreed that their institutions were turning out men and women who were more tough-minded. Where humor and humility are in short supply, it follows that humanity may also be lacking. That certainly seems to be the case with MBAs. One CEO notes, "Those young people seem intent on destroying each other to get to the top."

"There have got to be some people who go to the Harvard Business School and aren't ruined by the experience," says a partner at Lazard Frères. "But I have been watching MBAs in this business for over twenty years, and I have found a great majority of them immature in their judgments. They are inclined to make strong judgments without a background of experience and humility." Another puts it succinctly: "MBAs are not team players." Still others put it more directly—"ill-mannered," "rude," "brash," "impatient," "condescending"; the list of personal characteristics of MBAs goes on and on and gets no more desirable with length.

Some students have few social skills upon entering MBA programs and, what with the dominantly quantitative curriculum, little is done in the programs to develop social skills. Donald Carroll, dean at Wharton, admits, "Our system has a built-in tendency to reward the aggressive loner, so we get a higher number of relatively antisocial types who display a tendency not to suffer fools." Those who have a smattering of social facility upon entry quickly learn to set social niceties aside because winning is *all* that counts. Curtis W. Tarr, dean at the Johnson Graduate School of Management at Cornell University, sees the competitive, overly aggressive, opportunistic MBAs as a product of the classroom: "In theory, the goal of a graduate school should be to encourage each student to succeed. But in practice, the grading curve often rules. A few students will be judged outstanding, but most will be average and some will fail. In such an environment, students realize they must win, sometimes at someone else's cost. Cooperation gives way to tactics that guarantee success."[7]

Competition is the sine qua non of MBA programs. There is fierce competition to get in the best programs. Once in, students compete for limited spaces in the most desirable classes, with the star professors (who are themselves in competition with one another). In every class, students compete for grades so that they may compete for "rank in class" and thereby compete for the best job offers. All of the emphasis throughout the MBA program is on individual effort and individual reward; all else is sacrificed for self-interest. As one student explained, "You soon learn the fastest, surest way to an MBA is SYB, 'Screw Your Buddy.' "

On the job, this egocentric perspective translates into the insensitive, overly aggressive, job-hopping behavior that executives decry. It is precisely that sort of behavior for which the MBAs have been trained and, supporters argue, it is precisely the behavior they need to survive. The placement director for a major MBA program asserts: "If our students don't look out for themselves no one else will. In fact, they can count on other people taking advantage of them if they don't get the advantage first. Cooperation is a nice ideal but cutthroat competition is what's real."

The appeal for MBAs with a touch of humanity may be another case of business saying one thing and paying for another. As evidence, one cynical MBA points out, "I haven't heard of any recruiters asking to meet the funniest, most cooperative person in the class." Still, sentiment runs strong among experienced business executives that working *with others* is at least as important in business as working *against others* for one's self. Some MBA programs agree; for example, at Yale new students are organized into small working groups that stress teamwork. But few programs follow Yale's example, and the current of competition runs so deep in MBA education that isolated study groups or the occasional team project are unlikely to unleash a wellspring of more humane behavior on behalf of the MBAs toward their fellows. Whither goes concern for others goes also humility and humor. Short of major philosophical and pedagogical changes in MBA programs, complaints about the lack of compassion and civility of MBAs are likely to persist. The pedagogy of MBA programs comes in for its own measure of criticism.

Over and above course content and competition, the one thing that sets MBA programs apart from all other graduate degree pursuits is the *case method.* The case method originated at the Harvard Business School in 1924 and has since become the hallmark of virtually every MBA program in the country. A "case" is a written description (sometimes augmented today by video) of an actual business situation, often with the companies and participants disguised, but increasingly with full disclosure. Students read and analyze the case, then come to class where their analyses are prodded by the professor, where they debate with other students, and where they recommend a "solution."

The case method has some obvious strengths; it makes for lively class discussions and interaction, far removed from the droning of a professor spouting theory. The talented case teacher orchestrates the discussion like a Broadway play, pitting the students against one another in classic dramatic style with protagonists and antagonists while he alone holds the denouement, the knowledge of what really happened. Students are involved not only in the drama of the case discussion but in the *reality* of the case problems. They went to business school to study business and nothing quite meets their expectations like reading about the *real* problems of *real* companies and testing their judgment against what *real* executives did. Proponents of the case method believe it plays a unique role in business education, arguably bringing the student closer to the reality of management than any other device. One dean has said of the case method: "It provides an economical and effective vehicle by which the behavioral dimensions of administration can be sampled at the descriptive level. The case deals with a problem, a process, a decision, an event. In seeking to understand what occurred, the case writer cuts across the formal and the informal organization, the human and procedural dimensions, and the usual functional-jurisdictional lines. His is really an interdisciplinary enterprise, and his product becomes an important vehicle for providing students with a sense of reality."[8]

Powerful and pervasive as it may be, the case method is not without its detractors. Many of those detractors see in the shortcomings of the case method the seeds of what is wrong with MBAs and the myth of the MBA. Traditionalists argue that the case method ignores the basics. "It's fine that students take managerial accounting and learn why GM bought EDS, but when they get to the end of the course and can't tell a debit from a credit or know the difference between LIFO and FIFO, I wonder how much real accounting they have learned." The views of this Big Eight partner are echoed by businessmen and business educators and even students. An MBA student laments, "They tell us with the case method we'll learn the basics as we need to know them, but I can't help but think that there are some things I ought to know before I even look at a case!"

In defense of the case approach, proponents assert that business basics are covered as they actually appear in the real world—wrapped in problems. There is no doubting, however, that the case approach skips over some of the more mundane, albeit foundation, work in the business disciplines. As a result, MBAs are often poorly trained in the mechanics of management and, once on the job, they disdain the mechanical, detail work in favor of business strategy, policy, and the big picture.

The big-picture bias of MBAs is further promoted by the dominantly top-down perspective employed in case analyses. In virtually every case, the student is put in the position of the person in charge, the division manager, the senior vice-president, even the chief executive officer. Students analyze the case as though they see all and know all, and they examine alternatives as though they are omnipotent. Schooled in the CEO perspective for two years, it is only natural that MBA students take the same view into their first job. A recent MBA, now a real estate developer, reflected: "My first job was as a glorified gofer. In my whole MBA program I never once had a case about being a gofer. I kept wanting to look at deals from the CEO's point of view. No wonder people thought I was arrogant. I was. It took me a while to see the business from where I sat instead of from where I wanted to sit."

The omniscient, omnipotent CEO bias unquestionably affects the behavior of MBAs once on the job; they do often act as if they are the CEO. They also bring forward from the classroom to the company the simplistic, narrow perspective promoted by the case method. For all of their highly touted real-world complexity, cases actually deal with rather specifically defined, discipline-focused problems. In finance class the case will deal with financial problems, even though the same financial problems in the real world would be affected by the personalities and behavior of the principals involved, the perceptions in the marketplace, and a host of other dimensions. None of these dimensions will be discussed in the finance class because it is not a course in organization behavior or marketing. Real managers do not have the advantage of having problems predefined for them and isolated to a particular business discipline as MBAs do.

Robert Almon, Harvard MBA, describes his experience upon taking his case approach into the treasurer's office at General Motors: "At Harvard, you have two or three hours to spend on a case that might deal with the bankruptcy of a corporation," Almon recalls. "You get into the habit of thinking that you can deal with any problem quickly. In real life you don't have the luxury of skipping over details. That can result in horrible mistakes. I've been working on a financing deal to buy a piece of equipment for one of our divisions. On the first day we got a super rate; it was a great idea, sounded easy. Let's do it. Class is over. But the seller had never decided what the payment terms would be. It is very frustrating to have a deal go bad. Either you didn't protect yourself adequately, or you didn't think things through. You think very highly of yourself and you don't want to spend time worrying about boring details. But that is the way the world is. It does teach you a lot."

An additional area in which the case method is at least in part responsible for the behavior of MBAs is that of dealing with people. The case method approaches analysis and action as though management occurs in a vacuum. The MBA student analyzes the case, defends his analysis before and against the professor and other students, and recommends a course of action, with little regard for others and with absolutely no obligation to live with the consequences. Few managers would agree that this autonomous, even isolated, analysis and action approaches anything like the real world of business problems. As one manager described the case method, "It's like learning to drive by videocassette." Once in the job, MBAs behave as though they learned business behavior by videocassette, approaching their work much as they approached their cases.

Analysis and action in management is an *interactive* process— other people are involved. Problems do not come to the manager's desk predefined and prepackaged nor are they limited to a single discipline. Few managers, even CEOs, have the omni-science and omnipotence the MBA is afforded in his case work. In short, the case method provides MBAs with a distorted sense of business reality.

It is clear that MBA programs turn out financial analysts and consultants by the droves; they prepare students to analyze, liaise, coordinate, project, and all those other passive business activities for which staff people are (in)famous. What is not clear is whether MBA programs prepare MBAs to *do* anything. Eighty-six percent of CEOs polled by Louis Harris agree that "business schools teach students a lot about management but not much about what it takes to run a company." What it takes to run a company goes beyond managing information to managing people and managing things. At no time in their education are MBAs given responsibility for directing and evaluating the work of oth-ers. Without this responsibility, MBAs have no experience man-aging people. Even without any direct management experience, MBAs could develop some of the skills associated with managing others—communication skills, group skills, interpersonal skills—but coursework in quantitative skills drives out attention-to-people skills.

MBA programs not only neglect the basics of managing peo-ple, they typically ignore the basics of managing things—getting to know the business. The AACSB, the accrediting association for business schools, requires that accredited programs include at least one course in production and operations management. For the average MBA student this is as close as he or she will come to understanding how something is actually manufactured or produced. Consider this assignment from the POM course at a popular business school: "Compare McDonald's Corporation and Burger King. Also, select a third restaurant, take your family, and observe its operations. Select one of the three as the primary topic of your paper and consider the following questions: What is the basic process flow in each of the three restaurants? What are the major operational differences? How do these differences relate to each company's method of competing in the market-place? What implications do these characteristics (and differences) have for the management of the operation and for the future of these organizations? Be as specific and as quantitative as you can with respect to such issues as capacity, peak period, customer waiting time, and expected profitability. Generically, what is similar and what is different about managing service businesses versus manufacturing businesses?"

Here, two fast-food restaurant cases serve as foundation material for learning not only about restaurants but about the whole service sector! Actually, this example is one of the better ones. Most MBA programs treat production and operations as purely quantitative exercises, heavy on queuing theory, flow analysis, linear programing, quality control charts, and goal programing. As a rule, little is done with the service industry even though that sector is the primary employer of MBAs. MBA programs are not turning out managers who can design production or service or who can *deliver* it; they are turning out only people who can market it and analyze it. C. Jackson Grayson, chairman of the American Productivity Center and a former business school dean, sees the neglect of production as a problem a long time in the making: "American management has for twenty years coasted off the great research and development gains made during World War II, and constantly rewarded executives from marketing, financial, and legal sides of the business while it ignored the production men."[9]

Knowing production, be it production of goods or services, requires two things MBAs are short on—time and a willingness to get involved with the down-and-dirty details. Stanley Marcus writes: "Most of the young executives are so eager to be exposed to all phases of business that they don't stay in any one job long enough to develop expertise. Too many young executives know something about many things, but not a lot about anything. In their race to the presidency, many young executives lose sight of the fact that some jobs within a company take years to master."[10]

In addition to the time demands, learning a business from the shop floor up can be physically demanding. Michael Scott-Morton, professor of management at MIT, points out about manufacturing: "It's grubby work. You have to go through everything piece by piece. That's a level of detail that Americans don't seem to like."[11] Time-consuming, physically demanding, detailed—these descriptors associated with learning the business are not enticing to high-flying, fast-tracking MBAs. They find that the relatively quickly learned and, arguably, universally applicable financial analysis skills are much better suited to their ends, which, after all, are to get as high as they can as fast as they can and earn as much as they can along the way. MBAs believe that managing *someone* or, worse yet, managing *something* will only get in their way. MBA programs seem to agree.

With American manufacturing going abroad, foreign investment capital coming to America, and competition for worldwide markets on the rise, it makes sense that America's future business leaders would spend a fair amount of their academic preparation studying international business. But, as with so much in modern management, what makes sense does not necessarily happen. The dominant emphasis in virtually every one of the 650 MBA programs currently operating is on domestic companies and markets. When a program does advertise itself as having an "international focus," it means little more than that some of the courses use cases about multinational companies or that the student may take one course in international finance or international marketing.

Two or three courses and a couple of dozen cases do not constitute a focus on international business. Business schools must first acknowledge that much of what they teach doesn't apply elsewhere in the world. This realization could come by recruiting more international students and more faculty with international experience. The second major shortcoming of MBA programs vis-à-vis international business is the failure to give adequate (any) attention to alternative social-economic environments—the economics, social affairs, politics of countries along the Pacific Rim, in Europe, or in Central and South America. A typical case discussion about a company doing business in Brazil may give fifteen or twenty minutes to a stereotypical presentation of Brazilian culture and one hour to financing under conditions of fluctuating exchange rates.

Few (no) MBA programs avail themselves of the resident international resources elsewhere in the university. The MBA student exists in cultural isolation within the business school, rarely, if ever, venturing out to discover the courses in foreign languages, political science, international studies, or religion that might give him some true preparation for international business. A product manager for a major consumer goods company developing the South American market reflects on his preparation: "I knew I wanted to go international all along so I picked my courses carefully. It wasn't difficult, my school didn't have much to offer. What I did take ended up being pretty much useless. I quickly found out I needed to know a hell of a lot more about politics and family and religion than I did about international finance. Thank God I knew the language or I never would have accomplished anything."

Despite the acknowledged growth in the importance of international business for the success and well-being of American businesses, little has been done to internationalize MBA programs. The student who has an international perspective going in can pick and choose from available material that which he knows to be applicable. The student who doesn't have an international perspective beforehand is unlikely to get it from an MBA program.

These criticisms of MBA programs are by no means arcane or situational; they are well known, well and often articulated, and apply across the spectrum of business schools in one measure or another—from the "best," to the very biggest, to the barely business schools at all. The president of AACSB, when queried about necessary new areas for study in business schools, answered: "I think one that is certainly a candidate is the increasing internationalization of the world economy. Another would be the impact of technology on products, services, the way products are made, the way services are delivered, the way managers operate, and the way they react to competition. And I think a third way would be dramatically more attention paid to the interpersonal approaches to management."[12]

Knowing what to change and *changing* are two different things. The business community, the business schools, and the students voice continual criticisms of MBAs and MBA programs. In their own way, all are capable of rendering changes in the process and the product, yet the business community, the business schools, the students have not acted to bring about change. The myth of the MBA persists by benign neglect if nothing else but, as the many criticisms suggest, the effects may be far from benign.

Critics of the performance of the American economy over the last fifteen years are in general agreement that American business has placed too much emphasis on short-term profit and not enough on long-range planning; too much emphasis on financial maneuvering and not enough on the technology of production; too much emphasis on readily available markets and not enough on international development; too much attention to Wall Street and not enough attention to Main Street and the people who work and live there. It is more than coincidental that the reasons most frequently cited for the decline of the American economy mirror the most common criticisms of MBAs and MBA programs. Are MBAs the cause of the country's economic ailments? No, but the kind of thinking that promotes the value of the MBA and MBA training tends to encourage and reinforce the very elements that have led to the decline.

Research into responses to stress has revealed that in stressful situations, we are inclined to do one of two things: (1) we continue doing what we have been doing, harder, with greater effort; or (2) we do something completely different. Modern management has responded to stressful economic times with the first option—more short-term focus, more financial maneuvering, more market segmentation, more Wall Street, and, of course, more MBAs. Despite the obvious and well-documented shortcomings of this strategy, no one seems willing to try a different response in these stressful times for management. Businesses demand the MBA as a prerequisite for more and more jobs, at the entry level and on up the corporate ladder. Students continue to line up for every available seat in MBA programs. Business schools keep turning out "quant jocks" for staff jobs. In an attempt to dig out, management, through the MBA, is only digging itself in deeper and deeper. The mystique has created a morass.

The MBA has become a screening device for companies, a union card for junior executives, and a key product for business schools and universities—it has long since ceased to be an educational pursuit. The purpose of an MBA "to prepare the future business leaders of America" is realized only insofar as you have to have an MBA to get into business today. In light of the relative youth and inexperience of MBA students, coupled with the time constraints of a two-year program (of which fully one-quarter to one-third is spent interviewing for jobs), and the parochial nature of the business school professoriate, there is no hope of providing the comprehensive training required to truly prepare business leaders for the future. The list of educational needs alone is exhaustive, and when personal skills and intangible management "arts" are included, the preparatory task is truly insurmountable.

Realistically, the most that can be expected of the MBA—by anyone, businesses, students, or schools—is that MBAs have an ability to think and to learn about business. The business school, even with its vaunted case method, cannot substitute for the *experience* of managing, but it *can* and *should* help people to comprehend and cope with the experiences they will have, no matter when the degree comes in their career. If this were the case, the emphasis in MBA programs would shift away from training and toward education, away from how to analyze and toward how to think, away from detachment from others and toward involvement with others. The MBA should be the *first* step in a

179

continuing, lifelong process of management education and learning. Instead, the MBA is looked upon as preparation for a lifetime career, a one-time inoculation of training that forever prepares the recipient for managing in a complex, changing business environment. It is time to recognize that the MBA as currently constituted does not prepare people to manage anything, least of all their own learning. Nothing short of a full re-examination of the purposes and processes of MBA programs is needed if business leaders are to be truly prepared for the future. Management in America today is where it is in part because the future is here and the myth of the MBA has left business leaders woefully unprepared.

8

The Myth of Technology

Cyberphobia: fear of computer technology.

Cyberphrenia: addiction to computer technology.

In 1936, H. G. Wells wrote in *Things to Come* that technology would make man's unending struggle meaningful, ushering in the "triumph of human invention and human will." A little more than a decade later, in 1948, George Orwell had a more sinister view of technology and its effects. In Orwell's *1984*, technology exists only in the service of manipulation and repression: "Technological progress only happens when its products can in some way be used for the diminution of human liberty." There has never been a consensus on the effect of technology, not among utopian writers and certainly not among managers and workers. The cyberphrenics argue that technology will bring the true age of enlightenment, freeing workers and managers from the mundane, the trivial, the boring, and the stressful work in organizations, tapping into rather than destroying human creativity, and creating new jobs in the process. The cyberphobics counter that technology eliminates jobs, constrains creativity, and subjects workers to excessive control, regulation, and systemic stress.

The debate over technology and its effects is as old as this morning's rumor that every manager in the office will soon be getting a personal computer. Jonathan Weston, president of a consulting firm that specializes in installing computer systems in business, observes: "In every company we've ever gone into the situation has been exactly the same: half the people can't wait to get the machine on their desk and the other half figure they won't have a desk because the machine is going to eliminate their jobs. It's getting a little bit better but every time out you can bet that someone will ask, 'What can this thing do that I can't do better?' "

Twenty-five years ago, when computers were the size of a three-bedroom house and cost as much as an entire subdivision, the cyberphobics had a much stronger case. The price and practical applications of computers were so prohibitive that the decision to computerize or not to computerize was not an easy choice. The debate within companies was open to a variety of arguments pro and con, including the effects on jobs and the quality of working life. The new computer technology is such that in most businesses today the argument over whether or not to computerize is passé. Distinguished from earlier generation machines by (1) lower price, (2) improved reliability, (3) compactness, (4) increased speed of operation, (5) greater accuracy, and (6) lower energy consumption, the new computer technology has readily available applications to almost every area of every business. Cyberphobics may continue to argue the philosophical pros and cons of the technological organization, but they are talking largely to themselves. Practical considerations of competition and the driving need to lower costs have forced computerization upon managers. In computers, managers have found the answer to many of the complex information management tasks they face. Spurred on by successes in these areas, managers have looked to the new technology for help with other managerial challenges—motivation, leadership, communication. Therein lies the myth of technology. Whatever the improvements in affordability, reliability, compactness, speed, and accuracy, whatever the expansion of applications, machines cannot manage the key relationships among people that make managers effective—machines may even be in the way of managerial effectiveness.

The advances in technology today are truly astounding. In every discipline, science is pushing at the frontiers of knowledge; biochemical technology, robotics, medical technology—all can make a convincing case for being *the* dominant technology of the age. Insofar as management is concerned, however, it is "information technology" that has had and will continue to have the greatest impact. Information technology refers to the use of miniaturized electronic circuitry to process data. Information technology substitutes for or complements people's mental capabilities, in contrast to mechanical technology, which substitutes for people's physical capabilities. Information technology is symbolized for most managers by the computer.

The applications of microelectronics have proven to be almost limitless: new products and radical improvements of existing products; computer-assisted design and manufacturing; computer enhancement of service delivery in finance, medicine, retailing; computerized communications in the workplace. The new technology has already made possible new organization forms, new products and production processes, and new delivery systems.

Many American companies have adopted a new organization form by choosing to operate as marketing and distribution organizations for products made overseas. For example, Kodak sells camcorders made for it in Japan, RCA sells Japanese-made videocassette recorders, and GE sells microwave ovens made in Asia. General Motors, Ford, and Chrysler import small cars from Asia for sale as American models. Worlds of Wonder, the toy company, imports all its Teddy Ruxpin talking bears and Lazer Tag toys from five Asian factories. This strategy is possible, in large part, because of American leadership in the management of information. When your product is designed in West Germany, manufactured in Seoul, assembled in Juarez, marketed from New York, and distributed from dealerships all over the country, the success of your business depends upon your ability to use information to control and integrate these separate functions performed by separate entities in disparate locales around the world. The current competitive edge of American management is the mastery of the computer technology required to manage these critical information flows.

Lewis Galoob Toys is an example of the postindustrial corporation made possible by the new information technology. The toy giant with $58 million in sales of "action figures" is an aggregation of separate activities done in separate locales and linked by information technology. A mere 115 employees run the entire operation. Independent inventors and entertainment companies dream up most of Galoob's products, while outside specialists do most of the design and engineering. Galoob farms out manufacturing and packaging to a dozen or so contractors in Hong Kong, and they, in turn, pass on the most labor-intensive work to factories in China. When the toys land in the United States, they're distributed by commissioned manufacturers' representatives. Galoob doesn't even collect its accounts. It sells its receivables to Commercial Credit Corporation, a factoring company that also sets Galoob's credit policy. In short, says Executive Vice-President Robert Galoob, "our business is one of relationships." Galoob and his brother, David, the company's president, spend their time making all the pieces of the toy company fit together, with their phones, facsimile machines, and telexes working overtime.[1]

In the production process, increased control and integration are made possible by the ability to bring together a wide range of detailed information into one location in a timely fashion and to link physically separated people and functions in an interactive mode through a variety of computer connections. Computer-assisted design (CAD) and computer-assisted manufacturing (CAM) make it possible to rapidly adjust production runs with significant reductions in the cost of product changes. This offers managers greatly enhanced flexibility. The new technology contributed to improvements in product quality in design and in the ability to manufacture and test to more precise limits. Robotics and computer monitoring of workers allow for tighter control of production. Most significantly for managers, the new technology offers several possibilities for cost reductions: (1) reduced manpower; (2) more economical allocation of manpower;

(3) improved inventory information, such as stock levels, patterns of stock usage, and availability; and (4) reduction of wasted material and time in production. Cost reductions and standardized processes from the new technology are not limited to manufacturing. In the service sector, computerization makes it possible to form numbers of individual units into chains and to provide centralized functions by computer from a corporate office—inventory controls, purchasing, advertising, promotion, and so on—standardizing the production of the units, that is, rather than the units themselves. This pattern has been adopted by most of the successful service chains: hotels and restaurants, car rental agencies, movie theaters, real estate brokers, funeral parlors. Hertz and McDonald's, Hilton and Midas, Century 21 and SCA Services are good examples of the form.

The new technology has spawned a plethora of new products and services. Merrill Lynch & Company used computers to create the cash management account by combining information on a customer's checking, savings, credit card, and securities accounts into one computerized monthly statement and automatically "sweeping" idle funds into interest-bearing money market funds. Merrill Lynch has lured billions of dollars of assets from other places since it introduced CMA in 1978. It now is one of the company's most successful products. In almost a case study of how to apply the new technology, American Hospital Supply Corporation, which distributes products from 8,500 manufacturers to more than 100,000 health-care providers, set up computer links to its customers and suppliers. Hospitals could enter orders themselves via AHS terminals. The technology let the company cut inventories, improve customer service, and get better terms from suppliers for higher volumes. Even more important, it often locked out rival distributors that didn't have direct pipelines to hospitals. American Airlines Inc. has used computer and communications technology to build an entirely new business with sky-high profit margins. American provides its Sabre reservation system, which lists the flight schedules of every major airline in the world, to 48 percent of the approximately 24,000 automated travel agents in the United States. They pay American for every reservation made via Sabre for other carriers.

Even the delivery of the product and/or service to the consumer shows the effects of improved management information technology. Electronic point-of-sale systems (EPOS), such as devices to scan bar-coded individual sales items, allow for immediate and precise recording of customer flows, sales profits, and stock levels. This information can, in turn, be used for improved buying and inventory management as well as for more efficient deployment of the sales staff. An added benefit (to management) of EPOS systems is that they have made it possible to substitute part-time, less experienced employees for full-time employees, lowering costs and reducing the "headaches" of dealing with a full-time sales staff.

There is no disputing the opportunities afforded by the new information technology for increased control and integration, increased flexibility, reduced operating costs, and improved product quality. The experiential evidence in industry after industry supports the promised potential. Flush with the success of new information technology applications in the design, manufacture, and delivery of goods and services, managers believe that the new technology will have a similar impact on management work and the role of management in organizations. One assessment of the impact of new technology on management promises:

1. A flattening of the management pyramid by eliminating middle management positions. Because information is instantaneously available, there is less need for the management layers between top executives and first-line supervisors.
2. Improved decision making at all levels of management. Managers are now able to combine company data with outside information to get a broader perspective on industry-wide statistics or national and global economics.
3. Better organizational communication. Voice-store-and-forward telephone systems that avoid time-wasting re-

peat calls, and an electronic mail exchange that simultaneously transmits memos, reports and drafts, and teleconferencing to link remote managers to one another all help save time and cut costs.

4. Better scheduling, planning, and calendar management, as well as inventory control.

5. A 25 percent reduction in unproductive time formerly devoted to waiting for telephone calls to be returned, meetings to be held, and information to be sent.

6. The gradual replacement of operations managers by new information resource managers who study, analyze, and report on the newly available data, as well as coordinate the information support system.

7. More effective coordination of office and factory activities, including manufacturing, marketing, and finance, for better corporate team management.

8. Decision making pushed downward in the organization to first-line supervisors, who are better informed because they will have the necessary information in hand.[2]

There is in this listing and others like it the expectation that the new technology will answer many of the questions that perplex modern management—questions of size, efficiency, decision making, leadership, motivation (not coincidentally the areas where myths have the greatest currency among managers). Harley Shaiken, formerly of MIT's Program in Science, Technology, and Society, has said that with the new technology, management seeks "to bypass human input at almost any price." While this may be a somewhat cynical presentation of management intent for information technology, it is consistent with the applications of technology to production, that is, managers' motivation to "do away with the headaches." Certainly the new technology presents *opportunities* for change in the way managers manage *some things*, but it offers neither a substitute nor a salvation for the most critical of management responsibilities, those that involve people. The new technology is truly marvelous but machines can't manage; the hope/belief that they can is pure mythology. It is also a mistake to exaggerate the speed and extent to which the new technology will change management. It leads to an abdication of responsibility by cyberphrenics and cyberphobics alike. Such a reaction is clearly irresponsible; it is also quite unwarranted.

First, there is the matter of the speed and extent to which the new technology actually is *in* management. Here it is helpful to view current predictions of the "paperless office" with the perspective born of experience. When computers were first introduced to business in the 1950s, everyone predicted that they would completely revolutionize industry by the end of the decade. Of course, it wasn't so. The application of computers to organizational problems was much slower than had been predicted. It took several years to perfect lower-level routines such as payroll and accounting, and the more delicate and complex tasks still have not been completely computerized. It is true that today the pace of applications has quickened; yet the rate of the new technology differs widely across industries, among companies, and, even within companies, from function to function and from manager to manager. Currently, of the over 25 million managers and white-collar professionals, slightly more than 3 *percent* have computers. Of this number, it is safe to assume that a healthy percentage are idle much if not all of the time. Computer consultants call these unused machines (many of them early-generation PCs bought in the 1983–84 boom) "dusty"; managers are more likely to refer to them as "thirty-pound paperweights."

The experience in one food brokerage firm may be the norm in many of today's computerized offices. As the vice-president describes it: "We bought a computer system for what it *could* do, not for what we needed it to do. We were all dazzled by the possibilities. One thing it could do was allow every manager to link up from their own office to the mainframe, and have on-line access to all the company data. So, of course, every manager *had* to have one. Because the managers had them, the people who reported to them had to have them and so it went. We were a gold mine for the computer sales rep; we must have bought four dozen machines plus all the peripherals and all the software. I'd be willing to bet we couldn't find one-half dozen of those PCs even plugged in right now. I know there aren't more than three that are used on anywhere near a regular basis." This is not an isolated experience; the same thing has occurred in hundreds of "computerized" offices. Even *Fortune* was forced to conclude, "On a national scale, business's investment of hundreds of billions of dollars in computers and computer-aided communications has failed to bring about a discernible improvement in productivity."[3] The question is "Why?"

Even where the new technology is in place, improvements in managerial productivity may not be forthcoming.

An answer to the question of why the new technology has not appreciably enhanced managerial productivity is hinted at by the experience at General Motors, arguably the most ambitious application of new technology in American industry. In 1979, General Motors' management accepted the notion that "technological advancement is the single most important factor in improving productivity." They believed that if the company spent enough on computers and robots, increased efficiency would be assured; after $60 billion and eight years' worth of change, however, GM's new high-tech plants are hardly more efficient than the old ones. Analysts estimate GM's per-unit production costs exceed Ford's or Chrysler's by an average of $250, or 2.5 percent. GM's plants have slower start-up times than any other plants in the auto industry and they have yet to utilize their rated capacity. At the same time, at the NUMMI (New United Motor Manufacturing Inc.) plant in Fremont, California, where GM has participated in a joint venture with Toyota, new management practices have resulted in more efficient, higher-quality production than at any of the high-tech GM plants. The generally agreed lesson from the GM experience is that new technology pays off only when coupled with changes in the way work is done.

There is no technological imperative. Nothing happens *solely* because the technology is available to allow it to happen. Cars come standard-equipped with seat belts but fewer than 60 percent of drivers use them. Managers' desks may come standard-equipped with computers but there is no assurance that managers will use them. The way work is done, the way organizations are designed are the result of economic, social, and political (power) processes in an organization. The introduction and application of technology in a business are but one expression of those processes, an expression that is often at odds with the processes themselves, one of which is the nature of managerial work.

In 1973, Henry Mintzberg conducted a study of managerial work and discovered a general pattern: "The managers' days were characterized by a large number of brief, informal two-person contacts (telephone calls and unscheduled meetings), and relatively few scheduled meetings, which nevertheless took most of their time. Subordinates consumed about half the managers' contact time and were involved in two-thirds of the contacts. Other contacts were distributed among a wide variety of outsiders, many of them peers, associates, and co-directors on outside boards. The managers initiated less than one-third of their contacts, and only 5 percent were scheduled regularly."[4]

Subsequent, more detailed studies have revealed more specifics about managerial work. Twelve categories are generally agreed to capture what managers do: nonmanagerial work (exercising a functional skill); scheduling; ceremonies; solicitations from others; action requests from others; making requests of others; observational tours; receiving information; giving information; review sessions; strategy; and negotiation. The informational activities—gathering, analyzing, and transmitting data—taken together account for over one-half of the average manager's time.

Proponents of the new information-processing technology argue that it allows managers to be more efficient and more effective by reducing the time required for processing information. The managerial time freed could be spent on strategic decision making, evaluating, planning, and the other more productive pursuits. Viewed in this manner, the new technology can and should be the salvation of management. Many cyberphrenics have presented it as just that. Unfortunately, proponents of the new technology have not given much attention to the realities of managerial work. They have failed to realize that management is inherently a *social* activity, *not* a technological pursuit.

A manager's success is a function of how he or she manages *relationships*, not information. The time managers spend with superiors, subordinates, and peers is not a *means* to an end, as proponents of the new technology would view it (and an inefficient means at that); it is the end. Successful managers build networks of relationships up, down, and across the organization, relationships that they can draw upon to get things done. The time spent gathering and transmitting information—time that the new technology would reduce to electronic interfaces—is time spent *building* these important relationships.

John P. Kotter, professor of organization behavior at the Harvard Business School, has conducted an extensive, in-depth study of successful general managers (GMs). His work draws upon over 500 hours of direct observation over two years, and his comments on the "style" of managerial interaction amplify what is known about the content of managerial work and the importance of building relationships in order to get work done. Kotter notes that GMs spend the majority of their time working with others; in fact, less than 25 percent of their work time is spent alone. These "others" are up, down, across, and outside the organization as GMs pursue a wide variety of relationships and discuss an extremely broad range of topics. These discussions are very informal with lots of joking and nonwork-related issues in short, disjointed conversations. GMs rarely make "big decisions" and seldom tell others what to do or issue "orders." They do use a variety of techniques to influence others—asking, requesting, cajoling, and the like.[5]

These successful managers are successful because they recognize that the resources they need to get the job done include many people besides direct subordinates, inside and outside the organization, people over whom they have little or no direct control. Managers use information exchanges and interactions as vehicles to build relationships with those people who have the resources they need. Improved transmission, storage, accessibility, and analysis of information—all afforded by the new information technology—will not improve managerial work or effectiveness. Managerial work is accomplished through personal *relationships*, not through computer hook-ups. Managers might be made *more efficient* by the use of new information technologies, but in the process they would risk becoming *less effective* because of the reduced interaction with others.

There is an apt analogy at local retailers where electronic point-of-sales systems are in use. EPOS allow a retailer to record best-selling items, provide figures for instant reordering, highlight slow sellers for immediate markdowns, discount goods without changing tickets, and coordinate multiple-store merchandising, all while drastically reducing labor costs. What EPOS cannot do is get out in the aisles and help customers find products or answer customer questions. Retailers with long traditions of service, such as Sears, have essentially used EPOS to cut back on on-the-floor sales personnel. They have become serve-yourself operations. The new information technology in retailing has done wonders for merchants at the expense of service to the consumer by ignoring salesperson-to-customer relationships. The same "costs" to valued relationships have been hidden in promises of the benefits of the new technology for management; the new technology may actually cut managers off from the very relationships that are most important to their effectiveness.

One extreme of the technological attenuation of important managerial relationships is represented by the futuristic (cyberphrenics would say "realistic") concept of "home workers," or telecommuters. The new technology has made it possible for a number of workers to do their jobs at home and interact with the office through a computer linkup. Reports from some businesses suggest that as many as 75 percent of their employees could do their jobs at home, assuming the company provided them with the appropriate technology. The National Academy of Sciences estimates that by 1990, 10 million workers could be using office workstations in the home. Cyberphrenics wax positively poetic when they hypothesize about the benefits to managers of having their information workers at home stations. Among the many promised answers to perennial management problems are these outcomes of home workstations: (1) ability to use otherwise unavailable resources; (2) elimination of tardiness, absenteeism, and break-time issues; (3) reduced turnover; (4) improved worker satisfaction (and, therefore, productivity—remember the myth of motivation) because of decreased direct supervision, flexible work schedules, and easier family management. One proponent even goes so far as to see home workstations as the answer to many perplexing social problems: "Think what such a transition in the work force could do to urban overcrowding, traffic jams, and auto pollution, to say nothing about improving the quality of work life." In essence, the argument suggests that the new technology will make management easier and more effective by removing the manager-worker interface. If workers cannot be eliminated, at least they can be put out of sight!

There is no doubt that the new technology makes possible—through the home workstation—radically different arrangements between workers and managers. However, what is possible is not always what is *practical* or even what is advisable. This is particularly the case with management and the new technology. Experiments with home workstations have raised problems for managers that suggest that the new technology may exacerbate rather than ease managerial issues. Home workstations require new levels of trust between managers and workers who are allowed to work when and where they please without the usual managerial and organizational controls. The absence of requisite trust highlights discipline and performance problems, which become even more difficult for managers to deal with from a distance. Company loyalty declines with increased worker independence. Isolated from the organization, worker concerns for image and status in the organization, as well as concerns for their own career development, intensify, placing an additional burden on management communication. All of these problems occur in an atmosphere of social isolation for workers and, often, for managers, which is in and of itself stressful in addition to making the problems more difficult to resolve.

Some observers have argued persuasively that the social isolation that is a by-product of the new technology increases dependence upon effective managerial relationships by increasing the criticality of the technician's role. Mistakes by poorly trained, poorly motivated workers have been associated with the nuclear accidents at Three Mile Island and Chernobyl. Technological dependency increases the need for committed, motivated operators—behavioral requirements that underscore the importance of effective managerial relationships.

Experience with robotized factories, EPOS systems, home workstations, and computerized fail-safe systems underscore that the potential of the new technology to enhance management is limited not by electronic or mechanical constraints but by *social* and *behavioral* constraints. The link between technology and management has been proven not to be a deterministic link—the potential in the former is not an imperative for the latter. An excellent case in point, directly applicable to managerial productivity, is the highly touted "electronic mail" feature of the new technology. Electronic mail allows a message to be typed into a personal computer or a terminal and then transmitted variously through cable, telephone-cum-modem, or satellite link to a receiving personal computer or terminal. One of its alleged advantages is the so-called store-and-forward message. A user may send a message at any time and, unlike a telephone connection, e-mail does not require the recipient to be on the other end of the line. Recipients can access the stored message at their convenience. There are any number of logistical problems with e-mail: there are significant compatibility problems; among the dozen major competing services, none can be linked; and there is no universal director or e-mail central. It works adequately for internal organizational communication, but has limited application beyond that. In most respects, e-mail has been no more efficient than the telephone or postal service it is supposed to replace.

Computer companies are hard at work "debugging" and fine-tuning the e-mail technology to overcome the logistical inefficiencies. As is so often the case with the new technology, attention to hardware and software adjustments mask the behavioral problem with managerial communication—*what* is communicated. A survey of nearly 50,000 employees conducted by Opinion Research Corporation, a division of Arthur D. Little, revealed that fewer than one-half of all employees feel that management does a good job of communicating. Similar polls of managers reveal that they, too, consistently rate communications as their primary problem. The new technology is not likely to improve managerial communication in the eyes of workers who are far more concerned with the *content* of managerial messages. Chairman and CEO T. Mitchell Ford of Emhart Corporation of Farmington, Connecticut, a multinational with close to $2 billion in sales and 29,000 employees in twenty-one companies, said, "Technology may have revolutionized the communications process, but it's done little to break the lockjaw of 'counterfeit confidentiality' existing today in too many corporate cultures. . . . Openness, candor, straightforwardness in sharing relevant information with each other, with our employees, is the only way we can build and sustain the sense of union pivotal to our future growth."[6]

Openness, candor, "sharing relevant information with each other" are the requisites of effective managerial communication, the building blocks of effective relationships. Few would argue that the one-way transmittal of information via memo is the most effective way to communicate; no one would suggest that it is an effective way to build relationships. Yet the new technology offers essentially mechanized memoing—forgoing face-to-face or even voice-to-voice interactive give-and-take for terse, distilled messages typed by managers themselves (typing is a requisite managerial skill in the new technological age). Videotaped messages, or teleconferencing, are scarcely better. McLuhan was right: the medium is the message and the new technology, so far, means more top-down, one-way communication. Only speed is gained when the new information technology is employed; it does not change *what* is communicated; it does not improve the manager's relationships, or his or her relational skills, and, as a result, it does not improve managerial productivity.

E-mail may go the way of teletext (continuous transmission to a television set, à la closed-captioned text, with regular television programs) and videotex (a two-way, interactive system to allow for shopping, banking, and the like), new technology applications that are useful in a few specialized areas but which, in the main, represent technological achievements for which there is very little consumer demand. The same cannot be said of word processing and spreadsheet applications. These new technology applications are the most popular among managers, but they may have the lowest payoff. Indeed, to the extent that managers can get hands-on involvement with report drafting, designing report graphics, and playing with projections on spreadsheets through the new technology, it may be counterproductive. The new technology can be a distracting toy.

Bob German, president of 5-M Nurseries, the world's largest grower of crepe myrtles, says, "I don't want my sales managers spending all day deciding whether the sales report looks better with a bar graph or a pie chart. I want him managing the sales force. The worst thing that can happen is to give a perfectionist a word processor; all you're doing is encouraging him to draft and redraft with only marginal, if any, improvements in *what* he drafts. PCs are fine as long as you keep them out of the hands of managers."

Spreadsheets may invite even more abuses than word processing. Certainly the new technology and spreadsheet programing (such as Lotus 1-2-3, VisiCalc, Framework, and countless others) offer valuable means for managers to gather and examine important business data. The abuses of the technology come from endless managerial manipulations of the data, which are made easy, even invited, by these same programs. The result is the equivalent of the trivial messages that multiply in e-mail systems, known as electronic junk mail, as projections, and "if-then scenarios," which are run ad infinitum, ad nauseam. At one company, the controller's office was referred to by the division managers as "Lotusland." As one manager described it, "Our PCs aren't user-friendly, they're abuser-friendly. You can never get any help from anybody in the controller's office because they're all wrapped up in their scenarios. I can't seem to get through to them that I'm not in the business of managing projections, I manage products and people. If I could ignore them, it wouldn't bother me. But the real craziness is that you have to play their game just to defend yourself. I spend half my time doing projections on my machine so I can counter their projections. The idea of these PCs was to make us more productive, but I think they hurt efficiency as much as they help, maybe more."

Many managers and businesses become so enamored of what they *can* do with the new technology that they neglect to consider what they *should* do. It is a phenomenon that might be termed "technological drive-out" inasmuch as technology considerations drive out all others. In company after company, countless hours have been spent debating competing computer systems or alternative available software. The computer-based technology industry changes daily. The life cycle of a product averages three years; new products are introduced continuously. Hardware and software decisions made one day are often remade the next as management tries to keep up with the state of the art. The essence of technological drive-out is that decisions are driven by what's technologically possible rather than what is organizationally necessary. It was possible to build 747s so airlines ordered them; now 80 percent of those manufactured sit idle in the Arizona desert. The same thinking has characterized most business decisions about the new technology. The result is not only "dusty" computers but dusty systems.

Michael E. Porter, Harvard guru of corporate strategic thinking, has said, "Information technology can affect how every activity is and can be performed." This is 747 thinking, so reflective of how business views technology. No one questions that information technology *can* affect many, even most, activities in a firm but, likewise, no one seems to ask if it *should*. William Bowen attributes the "puny payoff" from office computers to this kind of distorted decision making. "In most cases managers do not scrutinize before they automate. They automate, then begin a sometimes painful learning process. One thing everybody who has been through it agrees on is that you do not get the benefits just by plugging in the equipment, even if it is the right equipment. The learning process often takes years."[7]

Still, most in management remain unconvinced and continue to look for the productivity payoff from the new technology. Economist Martin Neil Bailey, senior fellow at the Brookings Institute, has observed, "The puzzling thing is that the computer revolution has not yet paid off in productivity growth as did the earlier generations of innovations."[8] Hardware problems, software problems, managerial resistance—there are many scapegoats for *why* the new information technology has not been the salvation for management that was, and continues to be, promised. To anyone prepared to step back from the solution (technology) and examine the problem (management), it is really not so puzzling at all; it is the myth of technology.

The new information technology is more than a fad. James I. Cash, Jr., of Harvard reflects the sentiments of most businessmen and business observers when he notes: "The diffusion of technology is changing the way we do business and the way companies relate to customers and suppliers. This is no longer a technological phenomenon but a social one."[9] The technology is powerful, the applications seem universal, the potential limitless, and there is the widespread belief that if you're not keeping up with the new technology, you're falling behind with your business. The conventional wisdom of the computer age is that computers can and do change the way work is done. Technology has been assumed to be an imperative for the redesign of work and of organizations. With this technology-directed redesign, it has been assumed that there will be newfound efficiencies and increased levels of effectiveness for managers.

There have been just enough successes with applications of the new technology to assembly-line jobs, clerical work, and low-level administrative activities to fuel promises of the "new age of management" in which work and organizations are redesigned, eliminating the problems of management. To date, however, experience with the new technology has clearly shown that there is no work/organization imperative, *especially* for managers. This is not because of technological inadequacies, or logistical difficulties, or managerial inertia in adapting new technology, although these are all contributing factors. The real reason the new information technology has not resulted in changes in managerial productivity is that the new technology has little impact on the things managers do that make them effective or ineffective.

The new technology does not affect *what* managers do (or need to do) nor does it affect *how* managers do what they do, *nor should it.* If there are to be changes in the way managers work, the behavior must change *before* the supporting technology is put in place and the behavior must change *because* managers want it to. A consultant at Digital Equipment Corporation has captured the problem succinctly: "If people are doing the wrong things, when you automate you get them to do the wrong things faster." And, in the case of managers, spread the damage further. In fact, just as the use of computers to measure and control worker behavior often has a deleterious effect on productivity, so, too, the availability of new information technology often has a deleterious effect on managerial effectiveness. Managers frequently use the technology to get their informational needs met at arm's length to the neglect of building and maintaining the important personal relationships in their networks. There is no excuse for electronic point of management. People cannot be bar-coded. Managerial effectiveness depends upon building, maintaining, and utilizing a complex network of relationships up, down, across, and outside of an organization. Electronic interaction is no substitute for human interaction when it comes to getting managerial work done. A healthy perspective on the new information technology is one that views it as so much equipment—like telephones, typewriters, and calculators—which must be employed by people to have any productive use whatsoever.

The meaning of the myth of technology is that the questions "What *are* people doing?" and "What *should* people be doing?" are driven out by the mind-boggling possibilities of what people *could* be doing with machines. That is the technological challenge presented to managers today—the powerful potential of technological possibilities. It is also the myth.

A large part of doing business the way business needs to be done means managing without myths. *That* is the ongoing challenge to managers.

9
Managing Without Myths

We're in a helluva fix!
— *An anonymous manager commenting on the plight
of American business*

However, there is a danger here as well; namely,
of being drawn by one's dreams and inherited
myths away from the world of modern consciousness, fixed in patterns of archaic feeling and
thought inappropriate to contemporary life.
— *Joseph Campbell,*
Myths to Live By

American management is in "a hell of a fix"! This simple, de-
clarative observation describes a variety of conditions true of
management and managers today. Certainly the noun sense of
fix applies. Even the most naïve observer of business recognizes
the awkward situation, the dilemma, the predicament of managers today. Managers must balance competing pressures from
above and below within their own organization and, at the same
time, respond to pressures from the industry and from international competitors outside the organization. Often this means
managers must simultaneously pursue incompatible goals with
inadequate means. It is "a hell of a fix."

Alternative definitions of *fix* fit just as well. *Fix* can mean the
position found by taking bearings, much as a ship or plane finds
its position by taking a fix. American management today seems
to be searching for its bearings—alternatively looking to foreign
competitors, to consultants, to science, to technology for a reading on where management stands. Each reference point yields a
different position.

Finally, the slang use of *fix* descriptive of an addict's dose of a narcotic drug applies. Managers today seem addicted to simple panaceas proffered as remedies for whatever ails the business. However you look at it, management today is in a hell of a fix!

In times of distress and uncertainty, myths can be a source of comfort and direction. Myths embody our beliefs and dreams in stories handed down from generation to generation. Every culture has its own myths, and the managerial culture is no exception. Managers have their myths about the things that are important to them—organization, leadership, motivation, technology. In their current "fix," managers have increasingly turned to these myths for affirmation and for advice on a way to fix (repair) this fix they're in. As affirming and advising as these myths are, there is, as Joseph Campbell points out, "a danger here as well." It is the danger of being "drawn away from the world of modern consciousness, fixed in patterns of archaic feeling and thought inappropriate to contemporary life."

Campbell's forewarning is precisely what has come to pass for American managers. The mythology of management has drawn managers away from the realities of modern management and fixed them in patterns of feeling and thought that are inappropriate to contemporary organization life. As a consequence, managers' actions are often misdirected and their problems exacerbated rather than eased. Ever more perplexed by their inefficacy, the managers turn more and more to management myths for affirmation and advice. The cycle regenerates and the situation degenerates. Until managers begin to manage without myths, it will ever be so.

In this book, the dominant modern managerial myths have been exposed. New perspectives have been offered on the size and structure of businesses, leadership, motivation, preparation for business careers, and technology. These new perspectives have suggested new managerial responses to contemporary problems, responses more attuned to the reality of business today. Implicit in the new perspectives brought to these separate managerial issues is a new overall perspective on management, a perspective that both encourages and enables managers to manage without myths. This new perspective is embodied in four fundamental tenets.

More Means Less. There is a beguiling simplicity to popular management myths that belies the complex reality of behavior in business. Most management myths reduce the resolution of weighty management problems such as productivity, motivation, or leadership to a few simple steps that can easily be taken by a single organizational actor (manager) for the betterment of all concerned. Nothing could be further from the truth.

Even the smallest of organizations today represents a complex context for behavior. Multiple forces in and outside the organization act and interact in a dynamic fashion that defies reduction to simple causes or simple cures. As the size of the enterprise increases, the complexity increases exponentially. For example, questions of structure cannot be decided by de facto dictates to downsize and decentralize. There exist real, albeit complex, guides for the determination of optimum structure that have to do not with slogans but with considerations of strategy, scale, markets, and staff skills. Similarly, the decision of how far to go in the decentralization of decisions is not responsibly directed by the war cry "Radically decentralize!" The complexities of the decentralization question involve consideration of a business's need for control, coordination, and a comprehensive context as well as deliberation of the degree of confidence management has in subordinates.

Issues of participation and innovation are no less complex. The reality of modern management is that participation and innovation carry prerequisites such that the mere institution of participative and innovation-oriented procedures may not necessarily result in participative and innovative behaviors. Moreover, participation and innovation may not be necessary or even desirable in all businesses!

Seemingly simple structural solutions to the modern problems of managers are neither simple nor solutions. Structures result from complex social, economic, and political interactions within the firm and carry with them no behavioral imperatives. Because there is more involved in the selection of the appropriate size and structure of a business than mere sloganizing, such solutions offer much less than they promise—more means less.

The same is true of leadership. Today the myth of messianic leadership is held out to managers as a simple, sure cure for whatever ails a business. Iacocca, Pickens, Wang, Jobs, Geneen, Perot, and other contemporary corporate legends notwithstanding, there are simply not enough around to lead all the businesses that need leading today. More cannot be made, and we can't wait for them to come along. Even if there were a profusion of messianic leaders, it is not clear that the net effect of their visionary stewardship would be positive. Messianic leadership can damage an enterprise in the process of delivering it from evil. Looking closer, the leadership issue involves much more than savior solutions.

The dynamics of any leadership situation are sufficiently complex that there is *less* of a role for individuals—be they heroes or simply highly skilled managers—than modern mythology acknowledges. Management science has presented business with a mind-boggling number of leadership variables to be managed through the mastery of certain leadership skills and techniques. The net effect is that in a world where *everything* matters, *nothing* matters very much. It may just be that in the case of leadership, what matters most is not the leader but the *followers,* but this perspective is an affront to modern management mythology, which sees a central, critical role for managers. It is blasphemy to suggest that leaders don't matter. There are, of course, some things that managers can do as leaders that matter—clarify goals and paths, facilitate tasks where possible—but not nearly so much as they have imagined, nor with nearly as much effect as expected. The more we know to be involved in leadership, the less important the leader becomes.

Where motivation is concerned the theme of more is less is repeated. The more that modern motivation schemes move away from paying for performance, the less impact they have on worker behavior. A corollary to this point is that the more managers reward themselves, the less the impact of *any* motivational program on worker behavior. Until there is less in the way of disincentives, there is no opportunity for a more motivated work force. Individual motivation schemes, group programs, and organization-culture–focused efforts at enhancing performance all overlook these basics—disincentives and pay. Pep rallies, motivational programs, and sophisticated performance/productivity formulas give managers more and more levers to manipulate, but they result in less and less impact on employee behavior. Managers expect to be the "Great Motivators," but employees, who know that they alone control their behavior, remain unmoved. The most that managers can do is to tell employees *what* they want done and *how* they want it done, and then ensure that there is nothing to keep them from doing it. This, of course, is far less than managers would like to imagine themselves capable of doing to motivate employees.

More MBAs mean only more would-be managers with more inflated expectations of what they can do with analyses (not to mention their more inflated salary demands) and less attention to the management of people and products. Ironically, given the nature of most MBA programs, a more *degreed* work force may be a less *educated* work force. There is a corollary in the area of technology where the modern mythology results in more and more systems that are further and further from the nature of managerial work and, therefore, have less and less to do with what managers really do.

Managing without the myths requires that managers accept the fact that in management today *more means less*—more complexities of structure, leadership, motivation, education, and technology all mean *less of a role for the manager*. This is a reality that flies in the face of what managers have come to believe is their acknowledged and appropriate role in the organization.

The problem here is not so much the self-congratulatory behavior of successful executives, or consultants selling their ministrations to managers, or even MBA programs preparing young careerists to take a CEO perspective; it is the expectation these practices create in the minds of managers up and down the organization that they, with their magic, are responsible for the fate of employees and for the organization's successes or failures. As business fortunes rise and fall, managers, even supervisors, look to take personal credit or to fix the problem. However, business problems today, whatever their character—structure, strategy, motivation, leadership, technology—are so complex as virtually to defy resolution or resurrection by any individual actor *whatever his or her position in the organization*. Blinded as they are by the modern mythology of more powerful managers with more powerful tools at their disposal, managers are doomed to personal frustration and futile fixes.

The first step toward managing without myths, then, is for *managers to set aside their unrealistic expectations of themselves and their fixes*. Most of the behavior that counts in organizations cannot be mandated or manipulated by managers. In place of these expectations, managers must cultivate a sense of scale that allows them to perceive problems realistically and to take personal actions to bring about change. Managers must recognize paradoxically that less means more.

Less Means More. Karl Weick, professor of management at the University of Texas at Austin, has argued persuasively that thinking about social problems as "big problems"—in terms of numbers of people impacted or complexity or value discrepancy—renders them insoluble. "The massive scale on which social problems are conceived often precludes innovative action because the limits of bounded rationality are exceeded and arousal is raised to dysfunctionally high levels. People often define social problems in ways that overwhelm their ability to do anything about them."[1]

Weick's insights seem to apply to management as well. The prevailing myth of modern management is that the problems of

American business are "massive," so much so that they require nothing less than a total change in the culture, structure, and behavior of every organization. Fads and fixes offer panaceas for these pandemic problems that would have managers completely recast businesses and, thereby, behavior. All too often, managers, convinced that their problems are massive, attempt to apply resolutions of comparable magnitude, only to be frustrated and ultimately feel helpless. The problems seem so overwhelming—competition, culture, motivation, leadership, technology—and the experience of trying to solve them so futile that managers seem continually vacillating between ineffective engagement ("I must be able to make a difference") and total disengagement ("Nothing I do makes a difference"). As Weick points out, "When the magnitude of problems is scaled upward in the interest of mobilizing action, the quality of thought and action declines." This is the problem in American management today. The answer lies in what Weick calls "small wins," where less is more.

A small win is a discrete, concrete action of moderate importance—something specific and realizable. It can be either a minor improvement in something very important to the organization or a major improvement in something of less importance. The psychology of small wins—less is more—allows managers to reconceptualize massive, unmanageable business problems into small options over which they have, logically and legitimately, more control. With small, visible successes managers can create a feeling of efficacy for themselves and for their organization, attract allies, and lower resistance to subsequent changes. A series of small wins may even, over time, make inroads into massive problems.

The psychology of small wins has always been at the core of successful personal-change programs, whether it be weight loss, a personal savings program, exercise, or Alcoholics Anonymous's "One Day at a Time." Despite the successes of these programs, the notion of less is more has never been well received by managers, enamored as they are of immediate, far-reaching results and reinforced by the mythology of massive problems with universal solutions. "Fixing" has always had more appeal to managers than "fine-tuning." However, if managers today are to be at all effective, they must begin to think of the problems they confront in small, winnable terms.

A good place for managers to start a campaign of small wins would be with the orientation to fads and fixes in general. Although virtually every managerial fad has had an element of utility to it—from management by objectives to corporate culture—none live up to their promise of being panaceas. Managers have a difficult time taking what works and leaving the rest behind. The tendency is to buy the whole program, impose it across the board, and when the promised changes aren't forthcoming, throw the whole program out and put another one in. It is the massive-scale, "big win" mentality at work. Managers would be better advised to examine a fad, fix, or popular program of managerial magic for the *one* element, however insignificant, that seems to fit some dimensions of a problem at hand, use it, and discard the rest. Less will equal more.

An important dimension of small wins is not only that they lead to gains, but that they allow the preservation of gains as well. When programs to solve massive problems go out of fashion in a company, everything associated with the program—whether it worked or not—goes out as well. For example, there is much in MBO that managers found helpful, but when companies discarded MBO as being too burdensome, often even talk of measuring objectives was viewed as subversive. When programs are scaled down to implementing the pieces that work, there is less likelihood that discarding a program will erase desirable results that have been achieved.

The small-win mindset can be brought to each of the problems that perplex modern managers. Major structural transformations toward a more entrepreneurial environment provide a classic example of managers' massive-scale mentality. Downsizing, decentralizing, participating, and intrapreneuring—decisions to swing the entire company in first this direction, then that—ignore the fact that businesses are not so readily moved from one structure to another and, as a result, whatever the structure of the day, behavior changes very little, if at all. Managers would benefit far more from looking more closely at the structure of work nearer to their sphere of influence—starting with their own job, the job of their secretary, the jobs of those who report directly to them. Here, in the arena of small wins, decentralization (delegation), participation, and the encouragement of innovation can have a real impact on behavior. For most managers, the most profitable consideration of questions of structure will occur not at the level of the organization but at the level of their own office.

The case has already been made with regard to leadership that the appropriate behavior for the manager is to clarify goals and how they are to be achieved and, wherever possible, to facilitate workers achieving their goals. This is a much "smaller" role than messianic leadership or managerial leadership envision, but it is a role that is at once less frustrating and more fruitful for the average manager. It means, of course, setting aside both the glamour of moving the masses and the techniques of manipulating the masses for a more honest and humble exchange. However, in today's business climate, honesty and humility may be the stuff of heroes. The cumulative effect of small wins can most clearly be seen in the successes of followers of those managers who act within the limits of their leadership.

A small-win approach to motivation would mean that managers would look into the mirror and examine their own behaviors for those seemingly insignificant disincentives that spell doom for massive motivation and morale-boosting programs. Favored parking spaces, long lunch hours, health clubs, and the like will undermine any potential motivational wins regardless of size. Beyond winning over these disincentives, managers must reward the behavior they seek however important the behavior and however small the reward. If the manager's aim is to motivate an entire organization or even a whole unit, the magnitude of the problem is too massive to lead to effective managerial actions. But once disincentives are eliminated, motivation can be approached on a smaller, more manageable scale, even one-on-one if need be and one behavior at a time. With a small-win approach, every manager can be a motivator; where motivation is approached as a major problem, no manager can motivate.

After disparaging the contributions of MBAs to business, it may not need to be said that fewer MBAs in business will lead to more productive business behaviors by all concerned. There is another, perhaps more fundamental, application of the notion of small wins to the problems presented by the myth of the MBA. The attention American businesses give to the MBA credential in hiring and promotion decisions reflects an inflated sense of what one needs to know to perform effectively in an organization. That is, managers tend to hire and promote as though everyone in the company must be capable of being CEO. The result is that all begin to think of themselves as CEO and are relatively dissatisfied and less than effective in any other capacity (all other jobs, by definition, being beneath them). The concept of small wins, less is more, would shift the selection/advancement issue away from what people have done and what people are prepared to do to the question of what they need to do and what they can do *right now*. By requiring less, managers are likely to get more of the skill they need applied to the job at hand.

The temptation with technology, supported by modern mythology, is to go for the "big win." The temptation is strong because in the area of technology, as in no other area confronting management today, the big win seems *possible*. Computer systems can be imposed across the organization, technologically mandating the desired behaviors. However, experience has proved that there is no imperative in technology. Indeed, the more massive the infusion, the greater the confusion and the lesser the impact on work. Technological improvements ought logically to follow rather than force behavior change. This evolution is consistent with small wins. Managers need to ensure first that the necessary behaviors are in place, then look to technology to speed those behaviors. A steady succession of minor improvements where behavior change precedes technological support can move an organization far down the road toward maximizing its people and its processes.

Managers today typically define business problems in ways that overwhelm their ability to do anything about them. This managerial megalomania is encouraged by modern-management mythology. It is the source of many ineffective managerial actions. The second step toward managing without myths is for managers *to focus on discrete, concrete actions of moderate importance—to look for small wins*. Changing the scale of problems will change what can be done about them.

Some Things Never Change (and Never Should). It has become a cliché today to observe that "Change is the only constant!" Managers have certainly caught on to the war cry, so much so that one scarcely hears an informal conversation around the copying machine or a formal presentation to stockholders that doesn't note (in order): (1) it's a changing world; (2) we have to change to stay even and must change radically to get ahead; and (3) we are changing. Managerial myths rely on and reinforce the rhetoric of change with their models of managers as change agents forever fixing structures, cultures, motivation, systems, and their own behavior. Attention to the need for change and the need to manage change is certainly warranted—businesses *do* operate in dynamic environments, changes *are* needed, changes *are* taking place. However, the myopic fixation on change fostered by the modern management myths leads managers to overlook two fundamentals: (1) some things never change, and (2) some things never should. There are some constants in the managerial equation that management mythology frequently overlooks.

For all of the popular attention to megafirms today, the majority of us work in small businesses. This trend is on the increase. Employment levels in large companies are plateauing and, in many instances, declining. Displaced employees are moving toward opportunities in small entrepreneurial enterprises, particularly in the service sector. This trend does not suggest a constant—employment patterns are always in flux—but the way workers think about business *is* constant, and it is constantly in a small business context. All of us relate to the smallest identifiable unit of our work or trade. We think in terms of *"my* department," *"my* convenience store." It is human nature to reduce our experience to personal terms. This orientation is not likely to change. Managers must give up their megafirm mentality and focus their attention on the immediate, even intimate context, that defines workers' experience of the organization. What is constant here is the need for managers to get closer to employees.

At first glance, it would seem that there are no constants in the structure of organization. The current myth of entrepreneurial management with its emphasis on downsizing, decentralizing, participating, and innovating seems to be only the latest in an ever-evolving list of structural options. As implied in the discussion of "More Means Less," the often overlooked constant in structural considerations is that structure alone does not dictate behavior. Many managers, steeped in the mythology of entrepreneurial management, have made the prescribed structural changes; they have downsized and decentralized, created quality circles and skunkworks, then sat back and waited for employees to behave like entrepreneurs. But it hasn't happened. Employees continue behaving as they always have because the structural changes have not been accompanied by supporting changes in information systems, reward systems, selection and training, or any other of the myriad forces that affect behavior. Employees behave as they do in spite of the extant structure, not because of it; this is not likely to change. Managers need to focus on *what* employees do instead of *where* on the organization chart they do it.

There are really several constants in leadership that managers should keep in mind as they flirt with what is faddish. There is no denying that charismatic leaders are a constant in management. There have always been charismatic leaders; there will always be charismatic leaders. It is also a truism that managers cannot make themselves charismatic. Followers make leaders, followers determine *where* they will go and *how* they will get there and *who* they will follow. In most instances, it is the followers who will be there long after the leaders have gone on. The constant is that leaders do matter but not nearly so much as they imagine themselves to—what really matters are the followers.

The overlooked constant in the management of motivation is money, pure and simple. The modern mythology of management has generated a number of motivation schemes and schedules designed to get more and better performance without paying more. The reluctance of organizations to give managers discretionary decision power in the use of money as a motivator and the presence of significant motivational disincentives only serve to distance managers further from participating effectively in the motivation of employees. Money remains the most versatile and valued reward organizations can offer employees. All things considered, money may even be the most economical motivator available (i.e., measuring actual return on investment). This has been the case since the days piece rates were introduced at the turn of the century; it remained true when perks became popular in the fifties, and it will likely be true so long as there are employees. It is time managers recognized that the importance of money as a motivator is one of the constants of the managerial equation.

The myth of the MBA has created a false constant around the value of the degree when the true constant is the value of learning. In a sense this is yet another manifestation of modern-management mythology—focusing on *product* to the neglect of *process*. Managers do not *need* MBAs. Managers do need, and always will need, to be able to learn.

It borders on heresy to suggest today that there are constants in the area of technology. The nature of the technological beast is such that there is always something new—new processes, new products, new systems. What can be constant in an arena that dedicates itself to change? The constant here is that although the technology is ever-changing, the nature of managerial work remains the same. It is myth to imagine that technology will change what managers do or how they do it. There is no technological imperative; there is instead a managerial imperative. The requirements of management, the need to *relate* in order to be effective, dictate how the technology will be used instead of technology dictating how management will be pursued.

Throughout the preceding listing of the constants in management that are overlooked or set aside by modern management mythology there is a recurrent theme. Whether the issue at hand be structure or leadership, motivation or technology, the recurrent constant is the important role employees play in determining *what* managers do and *how* they do it. Modern mythology looks at management upside down! The mythical focus has been on what *managers* should be doing when the important consideration is what *employees* will respond to. Managing without myths means managing *with* employees. This perspective highlights yet another managerial constant—the need for managers to *listen.*

At several points, this treatise has touched upon the importance of the manager as a communicator. Too often, management mythology presents that role as the manager *telling*—telling employees about strategy, telling employees what jobs need to be done, telling employees how the jobs need to be done. Managing without myths means managers must *tell* less and *listen* more. Effective management today requires a responsiveness to employee predispositions toward structure, leadership, motivation, and the like. In order to be responsive, managers must open themselves to experiencing the organization as employees experience it—managers need to listen.

It won't be easy. Rarely noted for their communication skills, most managers compensate for their deficiencies by controlling the flow of information, both organizationally and interpersonally. Many managers view being open to influence by subordinates as a sign of "weakness." In addition to these attitudinal barriers to managerial hearing, there are structural and behavioral impediments. Managers are typically relatively isolated from their own organizations. Architecturally set apart (usually in a corner office) and buffered by a phalanx of secretaries and assistants, managers are seldom seen or spoken to by employees. Token tours (management by walking around) may put managers within physical reach of employees, but just *being* where employees can be heard is not enough; managers must *behave* in ways that allow employees to be heard.

Managers often fall into behaviors that actually discourage hearing from employees. Many managers personify the organization to the point that any criticism is viewed as a personal attack. Debating, denying, or discounting employee input are frequently used defensive tactics and certain signs of a closed managerial "ear." Some managers simply give the clear impression that they are "too busy" to concern themselves with what employees have to say. One of the strongest (and most lasting) deterrents to encouraging employees to share their experience is the failure of managers to act on undesirable conditions or practices that employees have previously brought to their attention. Once denied a "hearing," employees are reluctant to press the point. Fear of retribution (shoot the messenger) runs deep in subordinate/superior relationships.

With all of these structural and behavioral impediments to communicating up in the organization, it is a wonder that managers have any awareness at all of how employees experience the company—and most don't, but most don't see this as a handicap either. So long as managers rely on the myths of management, they don't need to open themselves to employees' perceptions and experiences. However, managing without the myths requires tapping into employee predispositions, discovering those things that never change by constantly listening and, in the process, discovering those things that *always* change.

Something Always Changes. For every managerial constant cast aside by the modern management mythology, it is possible to identify a half-dozen or more constantly changing elements of the managerial equation. Competition, markets, production techniques, capital availability, labor force skills, even relationships within the organization are all likely candidates for those things about business that seem always to be changing. Confronted with these continually changing elements, management mythology has made much of the importance of managing change and the manager as agent of change. The resultant fixes are ad hoc strategies for change, administrative adaptations to deal with the particular change(s) at hand, existing apart from normal managerial practices, with only sporadic success.

There is an alternative perspective on change that promises to be more rewarding for managers and their organizations than the prevailing mythology. It begins with recognizing that there is less to be gained for managers in speculating as to those elements of the managerial equation that are changeable than there is in accepting that *something will always be changing*. The former view approaches change as an ad hoc skill, a program or practice that must always be available to managers although not always needed, much like budgeting or succession planning. The perspective that in organizations "something always changes" shifts the focus away from managing change and toward *managing learning*—learning what is changing, learning when and how to respond. Managing without myths ultimately requires *managing learning*.

For all of the talk and writing in management today about new this and new that, changing this and changing that, the need for this and the need for that, there is precious little talk of learning and managers as learners. Implied in the fads and fixes is the sense that managers can simply acquire new perspectives and practices "off the shelf" and put their new learning to work. Would that it were so simple. Any change presupposes learning. Changing organizations must first be learning organizations, and managers of change must first manage learning.

Learning is typically thought of as the acquisition of knowledge and/or skills. In the case of managerial learning, we need to add behavior. Managers must know certain things, know how to use what they know, and use it. Managerial learning is not limited to the acquisition of new knowledge, skills, and behaviors, as it is assumed to be in management mythology. This *new learning* is only one variant. Managers may also need a significant amount of *relearning*—reacquiring certain knowledges, skills, and behaviors. For example, many managers would benefit from relearning what it was like to be an employee, which would better enable them to lead and to motivate. Finally, managers, especially today, need *unlearning*, the setting aside of knowledge, skills, and behaviors that are no longer appropriate and/or effective. Unlearning is a critical and frequently overlooked element of learning. Without unlearning—literally discarding knowledge, skills, and behaviors—new learning is simply layered upon an inappropriate foundation, and managers behave in self-defeating ways, simultaneously pursuing incompatible courses of action. Throughout, this book has argued that managers need to unlearn modern management mythology. Until this unlearning occurs, little new learning can take place.

It is difficult for managers to think about learning without making traditional associations with school, training, development programs, or learning from experience. Ask any manager how he manages learning in his organization and he will respond with a list of the training programs available through outside sources and through his own company. Whether or not these experiences promote any real learning is debatable. Training and consulting firms and university programs offer managers case discussions, lectures, videotapes, workbooks, and the like in the apparent belief that mere exposure to formula fixes constitutes sufficient experience for managers to put them into action. Training and development within organizations, growing to be the dominant source of managerial education, is scarcely better. Outside of instruction in narrowly defined task skills, most of what passes for management education is, in the words of one consultant, "executive entertainment," lacking any of the rigor required of a learning experience.

Schools and training and development programs are appropriate contexts for *some* kinds of learning—one can acquire new knowledge and skills (new learning) or relearn the same. However, few institutional educational programs, be they schools, in-company training and development, or external programs, give any attention to unlearning or to applying knowledge and skills via behavior.

Ask any executive how he manages his own learning and he will likely tell you how many years' experience he has and conclude with the observation that "experience is the best teacher." Experience is a fine teacher, but there's no assurance that managers will approach their experiences as learners, hence no assurance of what they will learn, if anything. More often than not, when a manager speaks of his fifteen years of experience, he's describing a single experience repeated for fifteen years, which he has continually interpreted as reinforcing whatever he knew going in. Still, experience remains the universal context for managerial learning—school and training programs being, at best, temporal and topical events. In large measure, a manager's capacity for effective action depends upon his capacity for learning from his own experience. Certainly experience provides the context in which a manager tests his learning. The management of learning requires a model applicable across learning environments, from the classroom to the shop floor, and appropriate to all learning agendas—new learning, relearning, and unlearning knowledge, skills, and behaviors. But most of all, if it is to be used by modern managers, it must be a model for learning from managerial experience.

There is a simple four-step model for learning from experience that has tremendous utility for managers and organizations. In this model, (1) a managerial/organizational experience is followed, by (2) processing the experience, thinking about it, talking with others about it, toward (3) forming generalizations or lessons from the experience, from which come (4) actions to take which lead to new experience.[2]

The simplicity of these four steps belies the intricacies of managers and organizations implementing this model for learning from experience. First, managers must be aware of their experiences. We all have experiences but few of us *experience* our experiences. Bill Torbert, associate dean of the Graduate School of Management at Boston College, has suggested that "there are four different but related levels of human experience: (1) the world outside, (2) one's own behavior, (3) one's internal cognitive-emotional-sensory structure, and (4) consciousness. We tend to be aware, to experience, only one level at a time."[3]

For example, a manager dealing with his employees may be so intent on what he is saying that he is oblivious to their receptivity/response, cut off from his own feelings, and out of touch with the overall sense of the exchanges. This experiential myopia results in managers leading and motivating as *they* want to lead or motivate without apparent regard for whether or not their behavior is effective. Processing the event at a later point, the manager's learning will likely be confined to what was said to him, since that was the level at which he experienced the interchange (the world outside). There is very little opportunity for him to act more effectively in subsequent interchanges because of the constraints on his learning imposed by his own limited experiencing.

In order to maximize their experience (and, therefore, their learning from experience), managers need to open themselves to alternative perspectives—*listening* to others. This can be as informal as asking others, "What was the experience like for you?" or as formal as focused group meetings with employees. Whatever the context, the key for the manager is to be open to the experiences of others. The same is true at the organizational level; processes must be developed for systematically tapping into alternative experiences of organizational actions, inside and outside the organization.

Processing the managerial experience should be framed in the context of a sense of the organizational constants. "How does this experience fit with other experiences? With what I know to be true about the organization? About management?" This processing should take place close in time to the experience. Managers must give learning the same priority as doing. The tendency of managers is to get caught up in doing, doing, doing, never pausing to process what they are doing so that they might learn from their experience.

From this processing there ought to emerge lessons learned

(new learning, relearning, and unlearning) and hypotheses to be tested in managerial action. The language of *hypothesis* and *test* is used here advisedly. If managerial action emerges from an experimental "if-then" learning perspective, it is more likely to be consistent in scope (More Means Less—realistic expectations) and scale (Less Means More—small wins) with managerial reality and more likely to lead to further learning as the cycle regenerates.

Learning from experience requires discipline on the part of managers. Managers must: (1) open themselves to the experience of others; (2) actively and purposely process their experience against their prior knowledge, skills, and behavior; (3) acknowledge their new learning, relearning, and/or unlearning; (4) test their learning in actions of appropriate scope and scale.

This model of managerial learning is a dramatic departure from the training and development that constitute management education in most organizations. Experiential learning is at once more personal and more pragmatic than conventional models of management education. Most important, experiential learning places the responsibility for learning on the individual manager, not on some external agent who makes a priori decisions about what has changed and how managers need to respond differently. By practicing experiential learning, managers can manage their own learning—learning what is changing, learning when and how to respond—having in their hands the capacity to deal effectively with those things in the managerial equation that always change.

What appears in these pages is the result of applying this model for learning from experience to modern management. In the process, myths have been exposed—myths about megafirms, entrepreneurial management, leadership, motivation, MBAs, and technology. In each arena the learning model exposed experiences of management reality that differed dramatically from the mythology of management. These experiences are neither esoteric nor ephemeral; they are the everyday encounters of managers in everyday business. The reality surrounds managers, yet the myths persist.

In large measure, modern-management myths embodied in fads and fixes are as pervasive and as persistent as they are because managers have not learned from their own experience but, rather, relied on being taught by others. Thus distanced from their own experience, their actions are distanced from reality—inappropriate to their organization, their role, their subordinates, their tasks. There exists within the experience of modern managers lessons for enhancing their effectiveness. Unlearning management myths will free managers from imagined constraints and the objectives they've chosen by habit. Learning or relearning from their own experience the messages in More Means Less, Less Means More, Some Things Never Change, and Something Always Changes will open to them unexpected opportunities to create the future—a future limited only by managers' capacity to learn from their *own* experiences.

Appendix

Answers to Forty Years of
Famous Fads and Fixes

1970s	Zero-Based Budgets	*1958*	Hula Hoops
1968	Nehru Jackets	*1960s*	Matrix Management
1981	Pac Man	*1980s*	Intrapreneuring/
1980s	Theory Z		Skunkworks
1950s	Theory Y	*1980s*	One-Minute
1955	Davy Crockett		Management
1971	Happy Faces	*1968–69*	Tie-Dying
1980s	MBWA	*1950s*	Computerization
1970s	MBAs	*1975*	Mood Rings
1950s	MBO	*1960s*	Conglomeration
1961	The Twist	*1980s*	Corporate Culture
1960s	T-Groups/Sensitivity	*1961*	Phone Booth/VW
	Training		Stuffing
1974	Streaking	*1953*	Slinky
1980s	Downsizing	*1960s*	Managerial Grid
1965–66	Go-Go Boots	*1952–53*	3-D Movies
1950s	Quantitative Methods	*1970s*	Participative
	(PERT/CPM)		Management
1981	Rubik's Cube	*1975–76*	Pet Rocks

1984	Trivial Pursuit	*1950s*	Diversification
1970s	Portfolio Management	*1956–57*	Poodle Skirts
1970s	Psychedelic Designs	*1960s*	Centralization
1971	Hot Pants	*1986*	Swatches

Notes

Chapter 2

1. Peter Drucker, *The Practice of Management* (New York: Harper & Row, 1954).
2. Douglas McGregor, *The Human Side of Enterprise* (New York: McGraw-Hill, 1960).
3. Robert R. Blake and Jane S. Mouton, *The Managerial Grid* (New York: McGraw-Hill, 1964).
4. George S. Day, "Diagnosing the Product Portfolio," *Journal of Marketing* 47 (April 1977).
5. Thomas J. Peters and Robert H. Waterman, *In Search of Excellence* (New York: Harper & Row, 1982).
6. Richard Mayer, "The Panacean Conspiracy," *Management Review*, June 1983.
7. Stanley Bing, "How to Live in a Fad Culture," *Esquire*, August 1986.

Chapter 3

1. John D. Glover, *The Revolutionary Corporations* (New York: Dow Jones, 1981).
2. John Welsh and Jerry White, "A Small Business Is Not a Little Big Business," *Harvard Business Review*, July–August 1981.
3. Interview, *INC.*, August 1986.
4. *New York Times*, April 15, 1986.
5. *Wall Street Journal*, January 21, 1987.
6. *New York Times*, May 25, 1986.

Chapter 4

1. *New York Times*, April 21, 1985.
2. *New York Times*, April 28, 1985.
3. Charles W. Hofer, "Structural and Strategic Alternatives," presentation to the Academy of Management, Chicago, August 17, 1986.
4. Ken Auletta, *The Art of Corporate Success: The Story of Schlumberger* (New York: G. P. Putnam's Sons, 1984).
5. *Wall Street Journal*, July 22, 1985.
6. *Wall Street Journal*, August 11, 1986.
7. Ibid.
8. *New York Times*, April 21, 1985.
9. *Management Review*, November 1979.
10. *INC.*, May 1981.
11. *Fortune*, June 21, 1986.
12. *Washington Post*, May 5, 1987.
13. *Fortune*, July 21, 1986.
14. Gifford Pinchot III, *Intrapreneuring: Why You Don't Have to Leave the Corporation to Become an Entrepreneur* (New York: Harper & Row, 1985).
15. *INC.*, July 1985.
16. Ibid.
17. Daniel Coleman, "The Psyche of the Entrepreneur," *New York Times Magazine*, April 13, 1986.

Chapter 5

1. H. J. Zoffer, "Training Managers to Take Charge," *New York Times*, October 20, 1985.
2. Ibid.
3. Lee Iacocca (with William Novak), *Iacocca: An Autobiography* (New York: Bantam Books, 1984).
4. T. Boone Pickens, *Boone* (Boston: Houghton Mifflin, 1987).
5. Mary Kay Ash, *Mary Kay* (New York: Harper & Row, 1981).
6. Harry Levison and Stuart Rosenthal, *CEO: Corporate Leadership in Action* (New York: Basic Books, 1984).
7. Charles Garfield, *Peak Performers* (New York: William Morrow, 1986).
8. Roy Rowan, *The Intuitive Manager* (Boston: Little, Brown, 1986).
9. John Kenneth Galbraith, *The Anatomy of Power* (Boston: Houghton Mifflin, 1983).
10. *Business Week*, June 23, 1986.
11. Irving L. Janis, *Groupthink* (Boston: Houghton Mifflin, 1972).
12. Galbraith, *The Anatomy of Power.*
13. *Business Week*, August 19, 1985.
14. D. D. VanFleet and G. A. Yukl, "A Century of Leadership Research," presentation to the Academy of Management, Chicago, August 17, 1986.
15. Alfred Sloan, *My Years with General Motors* (New York: Doubleday, 1963).
16. James O'Toole, "Alfred Sloan," *New Management*, Fall 1985.
17. See Harold S. Geneen, *Managing* (New York: Doubleday, 1985).
18. Wickham Skinner, "Geneen," *Harvard Business Review*, September–October 1985.
19. H. Edward Wrapp, "A Plague of Professional Managers," *New York Times*, April 8, 1979.
20. Robert J. Schoenberg, *Geneen* (New York: W. W. Norton, 1985).
21. Ellen Goodman, *Boston Globe*, October 14, 1986.
22. Donald M. Kendall, "The Four Simple Truths of Management," *Vital Speeches*, May 15, 1986.

23. *Fortune,* October 13, l986.
24. Warren Bennis and Burt Nanus, *Leaders: The Strategy for Taking Charge* (New York: Harper & Row, 1985).
25. Philip Selznick, *Leadership in Administration* (Evanston, Ill.: Row, Peterson, 1957).
26. For a complete discussion of leadership substitutes and neutralizers, see Steven Kerr and John M. Jermier, "Substitutes for Leadership: Their Meaning and Measurement," *Organizational Behavior and Human Performance,* December 1978.

Chapter 6

1. See Daniel Yankelovich and John Immerwahr, "Management and the Work Ethic," *Directors and Boards,* Fall 1983.
2. David Swartz, *Introduction to Management* (New York: HBJ Media Systems, 1984).
3. Arnold S. Judson, "The Awkward Truth About Productivity," *Harvard Business Review,* September–October 1982.
4. "Loyalty Ebbs at Many Companies as Employees Grow Disillusioned," *Wall Street Journal,* October 11, 1985.
5. Opinion Research Corporation, October 1985.
6. *The New Yorker,* January 28, 1985.
7. J. Richard Hackman, et al., "A New Strategy for Job Enrichment," *California Management Review,* Summer 1975.
8. Steven Kerr, "On the Folly of Rewarding A, While Hoping for B," *Academy of Management Journal* 18 (1975):769–83.
9. "A Noble Experiment Goes Bankrupt," *New York Times,* May 3, 1987.
10. Will Mitchell and Judith Kenner Thompson, "Through the Employee Ownership Maze," *California Management Review* 28, no. 4 (Summer 1986).
11. Terence E. Deal and Allan A. Kennedy, *Corporate Cultures: The Rites and Rituals of Corporate Life* (Reading, Mass.: Addison-Wesley, 1984).
12. *Wall Street Journal,* December 3, 1985.

13. Vijay Sathe, "Implications of Corporate Culture: A Manager's Guide to Action," *Organizational Dynamics*, Autumn 1983.
14. "Putting the Work Ethic to Work," *Public Agenda* (New York: The Public Agenda Foundation, 1983).
15. Morgan M. McCall, Jr., and Michael M. Lombardo, "What Makes a Top Executive?," *Psychology Today*, February 1983, pp. 26, 28–31.
16. Hay Group, Telesearch, "A Christmas Bonus Survey," December 1986.
17. Daniel Yankelovich and John Immerwahr, "Management and the Work Ethic."
18. *New York Times*, November 16, 1986.

Chapter 7

1. *Time*, May 4, 1981.
2. Personal interview with author, November 13, 1986.
3. Personal interview with author, September 24, 1986.
4. *Time*, May 4, 1981.
5. *Fortune*, March 31, 1986.
6. Personal interview with author, October 19, 1986.
7. *Fortune*, March 31, 1986.
8. Frank P. Sherwood, "Notes on the Development of Cases," Federal Executive Institute, Fall 1980.
9. C. Jackson Grayson, *Dun's Review*, July 1978.
10. Stanley Marcus, *Dallas Morning News*, September 19, 1986.
11. *New York Times*, January 11, 1987.
12. *Newsline*, October 1986.

Chapter 8

1. *Business Week*, March 3, 1986.
2. See Philip R. Harris, "Future Work," *Personnel Journal*, July 1985, and *Business Week*, September 29, 1986.
3. *Fortune*, May 26, 1986.

4. Henry Mintzberg, *The Nature of Managerial Work* (New York: Harper & Row, 1973).
5. See John P. Kotter, *The General Managers* (New York: Free Press, 1982).
6. *Forbes,* October 21, 1985.
7. *Fortune,* May 26, 1986.
8. Ibid.
9. *Business Week,* October 14, 1985.

Chapter 9

1. Karl Weick, "Small Wins," *American Psychologist* 39, no. 1 (1984).
2. C. Hampden-Turner, *Radical Man* (Cambridge, Mass.: Schenkman, 1970).
3. William Torbert, *Learning from Experience* (New York: Columbia University Press, 1973).

Index